Beautiful, powerful, and packed with t
for, *40 Days to God, My Father* is a wo
Whether you've struggled with trusting
Father or could use a reminder of His
rich dive into the goodness of God. Eacl
of who the Lord is toward us; Rosan
her reader to truth at every turn. I high[illegible] *Days to God, My Father* and look forward to giving it as a gift to the women in my life!

Ann Swindell,
Author of *The Path to Peace* and
Christmas in the Castle Library

This devotional is a much-needed breath of fresh air for any reader who wants daily reminders of who God is as their Heavenly Father. Rosann's storytelling coupled with scripture will encourage you as you seek to know God's heart.

Rebecca George
Author of *Do the Thing* and host of the Radical Radiance Podcast

40 Days to God, My Father is a deeply moving and powerful devotional that beautifully invites us to experience the heart of God as our loving and perfect Father. Through heartfelt stories and biblical reflections, Rosann S. Coulon reminds us that God's love is not only vast but deeply personal. Each day's reading offers profound insights that inspire trust, healing, and a renewed sense of peace in His care. This devotional will bless anyone longing to know God more intimately as the Father we all need, offering comfort and strength through every season of life.

Rachael Adams
Author of *Everyday Prayers for Love* and *A Little Goes a Long Way*

40 Days to God, My Father: Finding Shelter in the Heart of God by Rosann Coulon is a deeply moving devotional that invites readers to experience the tender love of our heavenly Father. With honesty and vulnerability, it addresses the "daddy wounds" so many of us carry, offering hope and healing through the unfailing love of our perfect Father. Each day, through Scripture, personal stories, prayers, and thoughtful prompts, it draws us closer to knowing God as the ultimate source of love, security, and trust. This devotional is a gentle yet powerful reminder that God is the Father who satisfies the deepest longings of our hearts—a Father who never fails or forsakes us. A must-read for anyone seeking comfort and healing in the loving arms of their heavenly Father.

Shelly Esser
Editor of Just Between Us Magazine

40 Days to God, My Father is a much-needed devotional that draws you back to the tender heart of our Heavenly Father. Through short, impactful daily readings rooted in Scripture and enriched with personal stories, Rosann reminds us of ten comforting attributes of God. With life-changing biblical truths to ponder each day, this book is the perfect resource for the New Year, the Lenten or Advent seasons, or anytime in between.

Shelby Dixon
Encouragement for Today Devotions Manager
at Proverbs 31 Ministries

In each devotional, Rosann Coulon invites you to go deeper into God's heart and enjoy His mercy, unconditional love, presence, and comfort. Her daily stories, coupled with encouragement through the scriptures, showcase our Heavenly Father's character. The additional probing application questions transform a short daily devotional into an opportunity to dig deeper into God's Word. Take your time with this devotional and learn more about His love for you.

Sharon W. Betters,
Author of *Treasures in Darkness, Treasures of Encouragement,* and Executive Director of MARKINC

Rosann Coulon's delight in God, diligence to study His Word, and dedication to leverage words to magnify the Lord makes her book, *40 Days to God, My Father,* a wise choice for any Christian woman looking for an engaging, biblical devotion. Rosann invites us to dive into the rich depths of our heavenly Father's love utilizing the Bible and hard won truth from her own journey. This is a devotion you'll want an extra copy of on your shelf to pass along to family and friends.

Jenny Marcelene
Freelance writer and editor for Living By Design Ministries

40 DAYS TO GOD, MY FATHER

Finding Shelter in the Heart of God

ROSANN S. COULON

CHRISTIAN FOCUS

Paperback ISBN 978-1-5271-1250-6
ebook ISBN 978-1-5271-1290-2

10 9 8 7 6 5 4 3 2 1

Published in 2025
by
Christian Focus Publications Ltd,
Geanies House, Fearn, Ross-shire,
IV20 1TW, Great Britain.
www.christianfocus.com

Cover design by Rubner Durais

Printed and bound by
Bell and Bain, Glasgow

MIX
Paper | Supporting responsible forestry
FSC® C007785

Contents

Dedication

For Mama and my sister, Angie.

Thank you for sticking with me through it all.
You've remained faithful to the Lord and our family.
It is because of your love, encouragement, and support
that these words exist.
I love you both.

HOW TO READ THIS BOOK

This devotional is made up of ten sections with each section having four daily readings in the form of chapters. While starting at Section 1 and reading through Section 10 is a great way to read this book, another option is to pick the section that resonates with your current life situation and start there.

You will get the most benefit from this book if you take the time to read the Scriptures and work through the Pause, Ponder, and Pray sections found at the end of each devotion. While I have thoughtfully and prayerfully written the words that make up each entry, I know that it's God's Word *alone* that transforms hearts and minds. Therefore, it is my highest desire for you to seek and search the Scriptures more than my own words. The Word is what our hearts need most.

Above all, I pray that every word within these pages awakens your heart to the deep love of your Heavenly Father—and His Word!

INTRODUCTION

Weariness, like a winter coat, weighed heavy on my soul. The plush leather couch in my counselor's office, often so inviting, offered no comfort as I sat for our session.

"Good morning," she said warmly.

My eyes avoided hers as I barely whispered, "Ugh," to her response. Tears immediately spilled down my cheeks as I wondered if these meetings were just a waste of time, and the constant tug-of-war for peace made me want to give up.

Sensing my despair and recognizing the short amount of time we had, she positioned herself closer and let her arrow fly, "Rosann, do you trust God?"

The word came out before I could stop it. "No." I gasped as the answer escaped my lips. I wished I could take it back—but any other answer would have only been a lie. She knew it and I knew it.

"It's no wonder you feel this way with what has happened with your father. But maybe now we can start moving forward."

My Earthly Father

On the night of April 28, 2018 my father (*my Daddy*) sank so low into the abyss of despair that he attempted to take his own life. Thankfully, by the miracle of God's grace, he awoke and called for help early the next morning. But if I am being completely honest, my dad had slipped into despondency long before that spring day—or at least the *Daddy* that I knew growing up. Why? Because substance abuse changes a person. For my father, it robbed him of his personality, demeanor, and thoughts. Shadows of darkness dimmed the source of his light for years.

My daddy had suffered from chronic illness for decades, and after years of taking medication, he succumbed to abusing and becoming addicted to that medication. Though he never took to the streets to support his habit, his doctor became his dealer, and he abused it nonetheless. His addiction broke our family, my parents' marriage, his job as a pastor, and all of our hearts.

And it broke something inside me, too.

While I couldn't see it at the time, I had built the foundation of my life on the security that revolved around my *earthly* father rather than on the love and truth of my *Heavenly* Father. The storm raging inside me as my father's addiction worsened had me sinking, swaying, and faltering—and I learned, painfully, that a house built on a faulty foundation will wash away when storms come. Psalm 11:3 asks, "If the foundations are destroyed, what can the righteous do?" I found that the foundation of my soul was not solid at all: it was like snow melting in the southern summertime.

An Honest Reflection

All of us have a "daddy story." Some are full of memories of joy and laughter, and they hold warm feelings of love. Others are expressed with sadness, tears, and feelings of betrayal. I have found myself on the spectrum of all of these emotions.

When my counselor asked if I trusted God, what I felt was that God had betrayed me. I felt unseen, unloved, and unsafe. Ultimately, I was projecting the feelings that I felt toward my earthly father onto my Heavenly Father.

After all, for most of my life, Daddy was the one I ran to for guidance, help, and reassurance. He had been a wonderful, godly father when he raised me. He taught me lessons in faith and life that stirred my desire for Jesus. But as the years of addiction wore on, his spiritual and mental vision became blurred. Though he was present in body, his absence became palpable. I could no longer turn to him for the guidance and help that he had offered me in the past.

I entered my first counseling session with the hope of finding guidance and resources to help my father. My plan was to fix him, and therefore to mend all that had been broken. I had no idea that the Lord had a different plan—one that was about *me*. It started with my admission that I didn't trust God and led me to begin, hesitantly, asking Him to help me trust Him fully and completely. God whispered to my heart that, in order to trust Him, I would have to know *Him* as my Father—and allow Him to be my strength, my helper, and my hope. This devotional is born out of that experience.

Our Heavenly Father

Throughout the Bible, God reveals His character. He is up close and personal in the lives of His children, and His Word is a revelation of the heart of God toward the people He created. Just as He was active in the lives of the saints of old, He is still the same God for us. He has revealed Himself as a loving, protecting, and guiding Father throughout history—and today.

While earthly fathers falter, God does not. In the New Testament, John says, "See what kind of love the Father has given to us, that we should be called children of God; and so we are" (1 John 3:1). By accepting Him into our hearts, we become His children—adopted into His kingdom and given all familial rights (John 1:12).

A Relationship Renewed

This devotional was written as a reminder—to you and to me—that God is the wonderful Father that each of us desperately needs. For as I have reflected upon the Scriptures, I have experienced my Heavenly Father pouring His perfect love into my heart. I am better able to grasp the depth and breadth of His magnificent love for me—and my trust in Him has been restored.

It is my hope that the stories within these pages, along with biblical examples of God as our Father, will encourage you to a newfound trust in the heart of God, *your Father.*

SECTION 1

A LOVING FATHER

DAY 1
He is My Good Father

If you then, who are evil, know how to give good gifts to your children, how much more will your Father who is in heaven give good things to those who ask him!
(Matthew 7:11)

A woman's voice crackled over the school intercom. "Please send Rosann Strickland to the office for early release." The words were music to my ears. I slammed the book closed, grabbed my book bag, and skipped out of my second-grade classroom.

I knew Daddy had gotten the note I left written across the white board on our kitchen wall. In large capital letters, I had carefully written: "I LOVE YOU, DADDY!" I had left the message right before I banged the front door shut and sauntered down our dirt road to hop on the school bus that morning.

School was the last place on earth I wanted to be as an eight-year-old. I had threatened to drop out several times since I graduated from kindergarten, but to no avail. And on the days I knew that Daddy would be working from home, each second spent at school was far more brutal. I wanted to be with him.

Strategically, I left colored hearts and I love you notes peppered around Daddy's chair, in his office, and on our white board to gain his attention. Each one was a plea for him to break me out of school prison to spend time with him.

Daddy didn't always sign me out of school early, but that day my heart sang as I rushed into his arms in that little elementary school hallway.

Being with my father was what I wanted more than anything in the world. And it is this longing—to be close with our Father—that Jesus points to when He teaches people to pray. In Matthew 6, Christ offers a prayer for us to model, and begins with the phrase, "Our Father" (Matt. 6:9). The Hebrew and Aramaic translation for "father" is "abba." This term for our Heavenly Father reveals warmth, intimacy, and loving care provided to His children.

Keeping this image in our minds, hear the words of Jesus in Matthew 7:11: "If you then, who are evil, know how to give good gifts to your children, how much more will your Father who is in heaven give good things to those who ask him!"

My earthly father gave me a good gift by answering my love notes with special time with him. Our Heavenly Father desires to do the same—and so much more. He wants to lavish us with His presence, His provision, His protection, and His will.

Pause:

Read Matthew 6:9-14; Matthew 7:7-11; James 1:17.

Ponder:

How does knowing God is a loving Father bring comfort to your heart? Make a plan to begin spending time with Him in prayer —and trust that He is welcoming you.

Pray:

Dear Father, thank you for loving me and welcoming me into Your arms. Sometimes, the difficulties in this life cause me to forget that You desire to give good gifts to me. Help me trust Your love for me even when my feelings betray me. In Jesus' name, Amen.

DAY 2
He Lovingly Thinks of Me

How precious to me are your thoughts, O God!
How vast is the sum of them!
If I would count them, they are more than the sand.
I awake, and I am still with you.
(Psalm 139:17-18)

I remember the first time I saw love with my eyes, held it in my arms, heard its cry, and smelled its wonder. It was the day my eldest niece was born.

After my sister endured a harrowing eighteen hours of labor, she was whisked away for surgery where this bundle of joy made an appearance into the world. And I will never forget that day.

My niece came adorned with a crown full of brown hair as soft as lamb's wool that I gently caressed with my fingers. As I held her closely, I inspected every appendage and whispered, "I love you" to her again and again.

I wanted her to know she had an aunt who would love her forever. Thankfully, my sister and her husband allowed me to be the doting aunt I longed to be.

Looking back on that day—and the days following into my niece's adulthood—I've watched her struggle to overcome obstacles and I've celebrated every accomplishment. And my love for my niece has remained steady.

Each time I think of her—and my other nieces and nephew—my heart dances on the inside. And though it's nowhere near the extent, this must be a small likeness to the Father's love for us—His children.

In my finite mind, I cannot come close to understanding God's love for me. I've even doubted it at times—and questioned it when His presence felt hidden in fogs of hardship.

But the words of King David in Psalm 139:17-18 are what I set my mind on: "How precious to me are your thoughts, O God! How vast is the sum of them! If I would count them, they are more than the sand. I awake, and I am still with you."

God thinks of me—one who is insignificant, unworthy, and incapable of any good thing apart from His help—and this boggles my mind. King David expresses how he's blown away by the love of God for him—each morning he continuously awakes to the steadfast love of God.

Friend, we have a personal—and conscious—Father who has us on His mind. He never forgets where we are, leaves us alone, or stops working on our behalf.

May your heart rejoice in the fact that your Heavenly Father *always* has you on His mind and loves you with no end in sight!

PAUSE:

Read Psalm 139; Jeremiah 29:11; Romans 11:33.

PONDER:

You are precious to God. How does knowing your Father lovingly thinks of you help your heart rest in His love?

PRAY:

Dear Father, I don't understand Your great love for me, but I'm grateful for it. Help me to remember, in the good and bad times, that You are always thinking of me with love —and watching over me. Fill me with more love for You. In Jesus' name, Amen.

DAY 3
A Melody of Love

The LORD your God is in your midst,
a mighty one who will save;
he will rejoice over you with gladness;
he will quiet you by his love;
he will exult over you with loud singing.
(Zephaniah 3:17)

I was slightly peeved the day I walked into the chapel at the retreat center. I came to this place on the mountain for a quiet and writing time.

My visit had started off serenely enough, but was interrupted by a large school group meeting. My plans were set awry by noise and the late-night banging of doors. And I like it best when my plans work out. When they don't, I fight the battle of frustration.

I entered the dimly-lit chapel in search of solitude to find a straggling teenager whose unwelcome presence, once again, thwarted my plan. A deep sigh escaped my lungs. Ignoring him, I strolled to the wall-sized glass windows to take in the woodsy scenery.

Lifting my eyes upward, I saw the partly sunny skies dotted with pocket-sized clouds and I silently prayed for

God to settle my weary mind. That's when instrumental music softly drifted from the keyboard and filled the chapel with joyful praise. My mind was instantly quieted.

Then I realized the music radiated from the fingers of the teenager whom I had just wished would leave me alone—the one who was inviting me into a holy encounter with the Lord.

I took a seat in the back of the chapel and closed my eyes. The whispers of a familiar verse from the book of Zephaniah echoed in my mind: "The Lord your God is in your midst, a mighty one who will save; he will rejoice over you with gladness; he will quiet you by his love; he will exult over you with loud singing" (Zeph. 3:17).

A tear slipped down my cheek as I imagined God singing a beautiful melody over me. I prayed: *Father, thank You for being in my midst—right here where things haven't gone as planned. You are singing over me with gladness, and Your love quiets my weary heart.*

That day, God's serenade drowned out my spinning thoughts of frustration. He reminded me that He is in control of my circumstances and loves me through every unwelcomed situation. And He gave me the grace to thank this teenager for giving me—what sounded like—heavenly music.

For the remainder of my stay at the retreat center, I shared the facility with the school group. So, the noisy interruptions continued. But when the battle with frustration threatened to overcome me, I remembered the sweet melody of God's love singing over me. And the Lord's presence sustained me to the end.

Friend, when your mind is tired of fighting against life's interruptions, remember your Father is in control of every situation. Those unmet plans may be the very place where God is orchestrating a meeting with Himself. Let Him quiet you with His love as He sings a beautiful melody over you.

PAUSE:

Read Zephaniah 3:17-20; Jeremiah 31:3; Ephesians 3:17-19.

PONDER:

Picture God's presence singing over you. How does this image help you know the love of the Father?

PRAY:

Dear Father, when my thoughts are spinning, quiet my mind with Your love. Let Your sweet song over me be louder than the roar of the circumstances surrounding me. Help me find solace and joy in Your presence. In Jesus' name, Amen.

⇝ DAY 4 ⇜

He Calls Me His Beloved

A voice from heaven said, "This is my beloved son, with whom I am well pleased."
(Matthew 3:17)

I hold a tattered index card in my hand and read the words scribbled across it. "You are my beloved daughter, Rosann. With you, I am well pleased."

At the prompting of a counselor years ago, I wrote these words to encourage my heart to rest in its truth—the truth that my Heavenly Father loves and is pleased with me. But I've often recoiled at the thought that I—so unworthy and undeserving—could be loved by the incomprehensible God who created heaven and earth. So, I ask myself a question: How is this true?

Since this handwritten note is a personalization of Matthew 3:17, where God says He is pleased with His Son, Jesus, I promptly search the Scripture for context and a better understanding to see if I can apply it to myself. After all, the Father's words here are spoken over Jesus—the perfect and sinless Son of God.

A detail I find fascinating is that God makes this statement before Jesus performed any miracles, died on the cross, or fulfilled the plan of salvation for mankind. Yet, the Father says, "I love you. I am pleased with you—and it is good you exist." And He says the same of you and me.

I struggle with attaching God's love to what I've achieved, how I've performed in any given situation, and whether I'm living the "good Christian life." Each time I fall short, I imagine God's love-o-meter plummeting like the quick release on a pressure cooker. But this is how the enemy works to muddy our view of God's true love for us.

The good news is that, when we accept Jesus as our Lord and Savior, we gain the right to be called daughters of the Most High—daughters He loves (1 John 3:1a). God loves us as He has loved Jesus. It is not dependent on our performance—or lack—and it is not defined by our circumstances.

Our Father loves us unconditionally. Nothing you or I do can make Him love us less—and nothing we do can make Him love us more. You, dear daughter, are the Father's beloved! With you, He is well pleased. Hallelujah!

PAUSE:

Read Matthew 3:17; John 17:7-11; Ephesians 1:3-8.

PONDER:

How does it help your heart to rest to know that the Father's love for you is not dependent on your performance?

Write Matthew 3:17 with your name inserted for personalization and place it where you will see it daily.

PRAY:

Dear Father, it's difficult to believe you love me when I feel so unworthy. Help me know that I am Your beloved daughter—and I am pleasing in Your sight. Thank you for accepting me, through Jesus, into Your family and giving me a love I never have to earn. In Jesus' name, Amen.

SECTION 2

AN ENCOURAGING FATHER

DAY 5
He Will Overcome My Struggle

"I have said these things to you,
that in me you may have peace.
In the world you will have tribulation.
But take heart; I have overcome the world."
(John 16:33)

I thought I knew pain before that moment. But nothing that had occurred in my life compared to the brokenness that I felt in my body, mind, and spirit the day I moved back home. After my diagnosis of Fibromyalgia and Chronic Fatigue Syndrome, along with a list of other disorders, I returned to my parents' home at age twenty-six because I could no longer physically support myself.

One morning I shuffled downstairs and eased into my dad's oversized recliner. Grabbing the remote, I surfed channels for something to help me escape from the heartache, disappointment, and anxiety about the future that welled inside of me.

It wasn't long before I noticed Daddy's stride coming my way. Stopping directly in front of me, he blocked my view from the TV screen and waited for me to meet his gaze. With tenderness in his eyes, he said: "I know this is hard right now, sweetie, but something good will come from it. God is in control of this situation." He turned and walked back out of the living room door—but not before turning my heart to the kindness of my Savior.

Jesus' words to the disciples before His impending death, resurrection, and ascension to heaven brought great encouragement to me during that season: "I have said these things to you, that in me you may have peace. In the world you will have tribulation. But take heart; I have overcome the world" (John 16:33).

I was walking through tribulation during that time, and in my pain, my first response was to wonder what I'd done to deserve it, and to wallow in my suffering. I had thought that if I served the Lord, my life would be smooth sailing. But I had it all wrong: tribulation is a normal part of the Christian life.

It's difficult to swallow Jesus' guarantee of trials in this life. And if we stop reading there, our hearts will fail. But hallelujah, He doesn't! Instead, Jesus pours an overflowing cup of hope into our shattered souls: "But take heart; I have overcome the world." He implores our hearts to rest in Him because He has already won the victory over this world!

Sitting in the recliner that day, I didn't feel victorious, but I *was* because I was in Christ. The same is true for all who are in Christ. No matter the struggle you face today, hold on to the peace of Jesus—and take heart, dear soul—our Father has overcome!

Pause:
John 16:31-33; Isaiah 9:6; 1 John 4:4.

Ponder:
Name the trouble that has unsettled your heart and take it to the Father. How does knowing that He promises victory fill Your heart with peace?

Pray:
Dear Father, when the trials of this life threaten to undo me, help me remember that You've already overcome every trouble this world can bring. I will trust You with my heartache and hold on to Your peace.
In Jesus' name, Amen.

DAY 6
With Me Wherever I Go

Have I not commanded you? Be strong and courageous. Do not be frightened, and do not be dismayed, for the LORD your God is with you wherever you go."
(Joshua 1:9)

Hesitantly, I peeked around the brick door of the conference room where I was scheduled to attend new employee training. I had moved four hours away from everyone I knew to take a teaching position, and although I was excited, I felt completely alone—and apprehensive about the future.

This world can be a frightening place. Through times of transition, long seasons of waiting or loss, it is important to have truth to cling to for strength, hope, and help.

One truth that offered encouragement to my heart during that time many years ago was God's promise to Joshua: "Be strong and courageous. Do not be frightened, and do not be dismayed, for the LORD your God is with you wherever you go" (Josh. 1:9).

God chose Joshua to take up Moses' mantle and finish leading the Israelites to the promised land of Canaan. I imagine Joshua felt apprehensive about stepping into his new role as leader to that vast number of people. Maybe he wondered if he could do what God had called him to do.

Yet Joshua did not have to face the task alone. He had the encouragement of the Father who loved him. God promised Joshua that He would lead him each step along the way—and that His presence would surely stay with him.

The good news is that this same promise God made to Joshua is also given to His children in every circumstance that we face. He is with us. We don't have to be afraid.

Thankfully, God's presence was with me through my first day of employee training and through every day of the year of teaching. He has been close beside me through every other season that I've walked through as well.

When fear and apprehension threaten to swallow us, we can hold on to the promise that our Father extends to us. And we can take courage because He is always with us.

Pause:

Read Joshua 1:5-9; Deuteronomy 1:29-30; Psalm 46:7.

Ponder:

What situation do you find yourself apprehensive about? How is your heart encouraged by the knowledge that God promises His presence with you?

Pray:

Dear Father, in times of apprehension and fear, remind me of the promise of Your presence. Fill my heart with courage as I follow You wherever You may lead. I will trust Your way and wait on Your time.
In Jesus' name, Amen.

DAY 7
All the Power I Need

"This is the word of the LORD to Zerubbabel: Not by might, nor by power, but by my Spirit, says the LORD of hosts."
(Zechariah 4:6)

I wish I could say that I have a love-hate relationship with exercise. But the truth is I have more of a hate-hate relationship with it, and it's always been this way. Yet anyone who has faced health crises or the years stacking up to middle age—or beyond—knows movement is a necessity.

This revelation came to me the hard way after years of sedentary living—brought on by prolonged chronic illness—left my muscles like mush. Once in recovery, I thought I could jump back into life where I had left off. But a forty-one-year-old body is a world away from a twenty-six-year-old one—the age I was when disability mowed me down.

As I began what I thought was normal activity, I quickly overdid it and induced severe back pain. The discomfort led me to therapists who taught me the correct way to carry my body and strengthen atrophied muscles.

I started attending a Pilates group class—and several months passed before I stopped contemplating quitting. One day in class, I watched my fellow classmates perform each move with perfection while my body sputtered and failed. I fought back tears and rushed to my car as soon as the session ended.

Dropping heavily into the driver's seat, I gripped the steering wheel. Looking up into the brilliant blue sky, I whispered to the Lord: *There's no way I can do this without You. Will You give me the strength to keep showing up?* I did not feel or see any changes from the months I had attended class—and I wondered if I ever would.

In the book of Zechariah, we find the story of Zerubbabel. He was tasked to rebuild the temple of the Lord. The original temple had been built by King Solomon during a time when he and the people of Israel had unlimited resources—including the strength of the people, a nation of power, and money. But this was not the case with Zerubbabel.

Perhaps Zerubbabel stood overlooking the rebuilding project and thought he didn't have what it would take to face the task ahead. But the Lord made it clear: "Not by might, nor by power, but by my Spirit." And by God's divine and sufficient supremacy, Zerubbabel completed the assignment.

Our Father's encouragement to Zerubbabel is the same gift He gives to *all* His children. You and I may not be tasked to rebuild temples, but we are often charged to perform duties—and walk through seasons—that require more strength than we possess.

For me, it was rebuilding a broken-down body—and it was beyond my ability alone. But the Spirit of God was present for Zerubbabel. He was there for me as well, and He will be with you too.

Maybe you are surveying an obstacle in your life that you know you don't have the capability to overcome. I have good news for you: Your Father has already provided His divine power to see you through to the other side. Let this encouragement strengthen your heart.

Pause:

Read Zechariah 4:6-10; Zechariah 12:10;
2 Corinthians 10:3-5.

Ponder:

What task are you staring at today that seems too big to overcome?
How does knowing your Father has the power to see you through give you strength to move forward?

Pray:

Dear Father, when I face difficult situations,
I often rely on my own failing resources.
Forgive me for thinking it's all up to me.
Thank You for reminding me that You
will supply unending power and unlimited
resources to see me through.
In Jesus' name, Amen.

DAY 8
Having a Heart of Peace

Peace I leave with you; my peace I give to you. Not as the world gives do I give to you. Let not your hearts be troubled, neither let them be afraid.
(John 14:27)

I wish my first response in a crisis wasn't fear, but peace. And I wish I didn't immediately spiral out of control when life falls apart or things don't go my way—but I do.

It's also true that I can mistake peace with having extra money in the bank account, getting a good health report, finding stability in my home, living in war-free times, and feeling secure in what comes with all of this. Sadly, when these things are not my reality—as is often the case—it can send me into a tailspin.

In my humanity, I'm given to trusting in myself and what I can see and feel. Perhaps it's the same for you. But we can cling to some good news as we walk through the uncertainties this life brings: a promise—and command—Jesus gave to the disciples. In John 14:27, Jesus said: "Peace I leave with you; my peace I give to you. Not as the world gives do I give to you. Let not your hearts be troubled, neither let them be afraid." Jesus extends these same words to encourage our hearts today.

When we place our hope, joy, and peace in the things of this world, we set ourselves up for disappointment and heartache. Good times are fleeting. Fear can set in and lead to constant worry over when it—whatever "it" is—will reach the end of its course and let us down.

But the peace Jesus offers is never-ending; it doesn't disappoint, and is far above what we can see, feel, and touch. This peace is a state of the soul—one resting in the presence of her Savior who holds the world and all its circumstances in His hands. And God holds you and me, too! He banishes fear and ushers true serenity into our hearts.

Friend, when everything around us is crumbling, we can lift our eyes to Jesus and cry out for His peace. Our circumstances may not change, but our hearts can be filled with His priceless peace and our souls can proclaim, "It is well"—even when, by worldly standards, everything is on fire. May we hold tightly to this encouragement today and never let it go.

Pause:

Read John 14:27-31; Philippians 4:6-7; Colossians 3:15.

Ponder:

In what things of this world have you sought to find peace? What are some steps you can take to seek the peace only Jesus offers?

Pray:

Dear Father, forgive me for seeking peace in this world. Help me remember complete peace is found in You alone. May this truth banish my fears and settle my heart.
Thank You for this gift.
In Jesus' name, Amen.

SECTION 3

A FAITHFUL FATHER

DAY 9
The One Who Never Fails

Let us hold fast the confession of our hope without wavering, for he who promised is faithful.
(Hebrews 10:23)

There was something that I could always count on growing up: when dinner was served, all our family would gather around the table to receive it. Daddy took his place at the head and Mama sat at the opposite end. My brother, sister, and I filled the chairs in-between.

"Precious Father, thank You for this food and bless it for the nourishment of our bodies." Daddy's prayer of blessing rang with familiarity every night. And once the steaming biscuits were served, Daddy went around the table one-by-one, inquiring, "How was your day?" He genuinely wanted to know how each of his children was doing, and our conversation revolved around school events and family updates. This occurrence was what I knew I could expect—and rely on—nearly every night of the week.

Because of this daily routine, I never questioned Daddy's interest and presence in my life. Whether I had a hard day at school, a squabble with a friend, or needed advice, I was sure to get to talk it out with Daddy. I was certain of his support and love for me throughout the years because he proved himself faithful to me by simply being dependable.

God is even more dependable than the most consistent father. He is faithful to us through every season and circumstance. The author of Hebrews points to this truth through the exhortation given to the saints to: "Hold fast the confession of our hope without wavering, for he who promised is faithful" (Heb. 10:23). Just as a newborn baby reflexively clamps down on an extended finger, we—as God's children—can grip the truth of God's faithfulness and "hold fast" to Him, assured that He will not fail us.

Truthfully, as I've walked the road to adulthood, there are hard facts I've had to accept about humanity. One fact is that there is no person—my Daddy included—who can remain perfectly reliable and faithful. Sometimes it's because of circumstances outside of a person's control that hinder a promise from being fulfilled: sometimes it's their fallen flesh that brings about their broken promises.

But this is never the case with God! We can have full confidence that every promise He gives will be fulfilled. Over and over again, He has proven Himself faithful to accomplish His Word (Isa. 55:11; Heb. 13:8). Friend, you can rely on Your Heavenly Father without wavering. He cannot fail! Each day and every moment, He is present and available in your life. Never let go of this truth.

Pause:
Read Hebrews 10:23; 1 Thessalonians 5:24; Psalm 145:13.

Ponder:
Take a moment to search your heart for hurts brought about by those who have let you down. How does knowing that God is Your faithful Father help to heal this pain?

Pray:
Dear Father, thank You for Your faithfulness. When circumstances surrounding me cause me to doubt—and when others let me down—help me hold fast to this truth and refuse to let go. Fill me with hope as I rest in Your faithfulness. In Jesus' name, Amen.

DAY 10
Clinging to Truth

The steadfast love of the Lord never ceases;
his mercies never come to an end;
they are new every morning;
great is your faithfulness.
(Lamentations 3:22-23)

I stood peering out the glass storm door and watched two cardinals flit across the sky like crimson sparkles. As the summer temperature outside my home climbed, so did my pain level. My headaches were exacerbated by the humidity, so I didn't dare cross the threshold. But after several days battling body aches, I felt stuck inside. The intense heat had already lingered for weeks and no end was in sight.

That's when I heard the continual swooshing of passing cars at the end of my driveway. My house was on a popular route to destinations by the sea. I guessed the increased traffic meant families were fulfilling plans to vacation at beaches in the surrounding area. But I had no such plans—and it felt like I never would.

I shifted to lean my shoulder against the doorjamb to rest my pounding head. Sadness for my long-enduring trial—and grief for all I was missing—fell heavy on my heart. As a tear escaped down my cheek, I allowed myself to weep for all my disappointments.

In the Bible, the prophet Jeremiah was also familiar with pain, despair, and weeping. He is even referred to as the "weeping prophet." During his great grief, he penned the book of Lamentations—considered by some to be the saddest book of the Bible. Jeremiah warned the people of Jerusalem destruction was coming if they didn't turn their hearts back to God, yet few listened. The impending judgment became reality when the Babylonians broke down the city's walls, slaughtered God's people, and destroyed the temple.

In the middle of his sad recordings, Jeremiah makes a profound statement: "But this I call to mind, and therefore I have hope: The steadfast love of the LORD never ceases; his mercies never come to an end; they are new every morning; great is your faithfulness" (Lam. 3:22-23).

Amid his pain and disappointment, Jeremiah reminded himself of God's faithfulness and turned his heart back to hope. I clung to this same truth on that day years ago, grieving the damage from lingering hardship. Even today, I continue to return to the truth of God's unchanging character when the walls of my heart are shattered and dreams turn to dust.

God's love is beyond our comprehension. His compassion is boundless. Every morning, He brings new blessings. He cannot change and His faithfulness is steadfast—always was, is, and will be. Hold on to the hope you have in Him, dear friend. He will never disappoint!

PAUSE:
Read Lamentations 3:20-26; Psalm 73:26; Hebrews 6:18.

PONDER:
What situation brings tears to your heart? How does knowing God is faithful fill you with hope as you endure?

PRAY:
Dear Father, thank You for Your love and mercy. I praise You for Your unending faithfulness that carries me through the hardest trials in this life. Fill me with hope as I hold on to Your promises. In Jesus' name, Amen.

DAY 11
When Hard Times Linger

And the LORD was with Joseph.
(Genesis 39:2)

I've read (or heard) Joseph's story in the Bible more times than I can count. Yet I vividly remember the first time I read all the details surrounding it. In my teens, I took on the challenge to read the Bible in a year. Hot tears streamed down my face as I read how Joseph's brothers sold him into slavery.

Questions stormed my mind. *How could they do that to him? What did Joseph feel when his brothers turned their backs on him?* Then, when it seemed Joseph's life was on an upward climb, something terrible happened again. He was falsely accused and sent to prison—where he had an extended stay. With all the ups and downs Joseph experienced, I wonder if he ever asked the Lord, "How long must I endure this trial?"

It's easy to question God when betrayal, heartache, pain, and misunderstanding linger—sometimes for years on end. I've been there. When chronic illness shattered my dreams, financial hardship was a constant companion, and my father's drug abuse stole years of joy from my family, I asked, "Where are You in all of this, Lord?"

During times when my heart was ripped apart, I found great assurance in these words: "And the LORD was with Joseph" (Gen. 39:2). When Joseph's brothers tossed him into a pit, the Lord was with him. When Potiphar falsely accused Joseph and locked him in prison, the Lord was with him. When God freed Joseph from prison, made him ruler in Egypt, and reunited Joseph with his family, the Lord was with him.

God's faithful hand had penned Joseph's story every step along the way. God never once left Joseph's side, forgot him, or stopped working on his behalf. Our Father does the same for you and me. Through it all, He remains faithful.

Joseph told his brothers: "you meant evil against me, but God meant it for good" (Gen. 50:20). And we can say the same about the trials we endure. Our enemy has evil intentions. He wants us to doubt God's goodness and destroy our hope. But our Father remains faithful through every trial, no matter how long it lasts—and He will bring beauty from the pain.

Dear friend, don't give up—or succumb to despair. Your Father is with you. He will never leave you. And He will bring an end to every trial—even if it's on the other side of this life on earth. Take heart: His faithfulness is sure!

Pause:

Read Genesis 37-41; Psalm 105; Romans 8:28.

Ponder:

Make a list of ways God has proven Himself faithful to you in the past. How does focusing on His past faithfulness help you trust His faithfulness for the future?

Pray:

Dear Father, when I live in prolonged trials, it's easy for me to question if Your presence is with me—and how You're working in my life. Forgive me for doubting You. Thank You for remaining faithful always.
In Jesus' name, Amen.

DAY 12
Even When I Cannot See

By faith Sarah herself received power to conceive, even when she was past the age, since she considered him faithful who had promised.
(Hebrews 11:11)

Torrential rain pelted my car's windshield as a flash of lightning sizzled across the sky. Dropping my speed to a slow creep, I gripped the steering wheel so tightly that pain shot through my hands. *Lord, help me.* The words echoed repeatedly.

After the taillights from the car ahead were no longer visible and the road disappeared, I decided to pull over to the shoulder of the highway. Miles from home, alone, and afraid, I had no idea when I would arrive to my destination. I couldn't see how it was possible since the road seemed to have vanished.

I felt anxiety tighten like a band around my chest. With the storm swirling around me, I knew I had to make a choice.

I could choose to trust God's faithfulness in the middle of the storm surrounding me or allow fear to drown out the truth of His character—and paralyze me from ever moving forward. It's the same choice I've had to make amid lingering years of chronic illness, seasons of job loss, long years of my father's struggle with substance abuse, and countless other difficulties.

Perhaps Sarah had a similar defining moment. God promised that she would conceive a child, yet decades passed without any sign of the promise's fulfillment. And when Sarah's barrenness extended beyond her child-bearing years, she was left waiting in clouds of uncertainty without knowing when—or how—God would complete His plan.

Yet even in this seemingly impossible circumstance, Sarah chose to trust God. She "considered him faithful who had promised" (Heb. 11:11) and God proved Himself faithful by gifting Sarah and Abraham a son, Isaac—the heir who made Abraham the "father of many nations" (Gen. 17:5).

Whatever we face—whether torrential downpours on the highway or the pain of infertility or the many other trials we can walk through—we have a choice to make in the midst of our storms. Will we choose to trust God or let the storm drown out His voice?

With His Word and the help of the Holy Spirit, the good news is that we can always make the choice to stand on the faithfulness of our Father. Just as He performed His promise to Sarah, He will keep all His promises to us. Our great Father promises to see us through this life to the very end. May we always consider Him faithful.

Pause:

Read Hebrews 11:11; Genesis 18:11-14; Romans 4:20-21.

Ponder:

Is there a situation you're facing that fills you with uncertainty? How does believing that God is faithful give you strength to trust that He will deliver you?

Pray:

Dear Father, thank you for reminding me of Your faithfulness. Forgive me for the times I doubted that You would see me through. Fill me with peace as I face the storms of life and help me daily choose to believe that You are my faithful Father.
In Jesus' name, Amen.

SECTION 4

A GUIDING FATHER

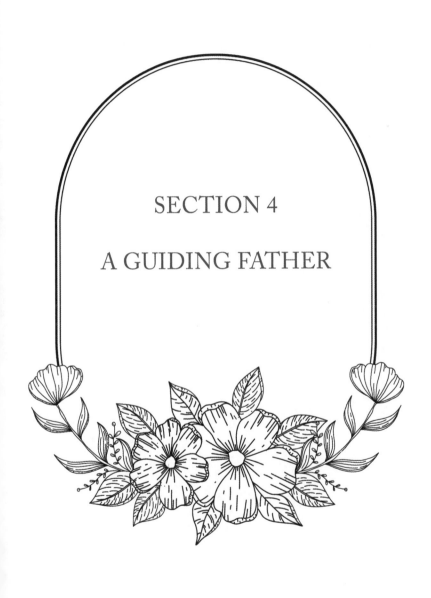

DAY 13
Follow in His Footsteps

He leads me in paths of righteousness
for His name's sake.
(Psalm 23:3b)

I'm five years old, walking down the long dirt road of my childhood home with sand stuck between my toes, following behind my father. My mouth is set to one side as I try, with all my might, to get my tiny feet to step into his size eleven footprints ahead. His long legs make the footprints too far apart for me to land exactly where he lands, so I begin jumping from one footprint to the next. Determination wills me to follow in his path.

This particular path leads to his personal sanctuary—an outbuilding at the end of the drive that serves as his home office. It is the place assigned for him to steal time away to meet privately with God, study His Word, and pray. He is a pastor, a father, a husband, and a leader. Even at the age of five, I understand that this is Daddy's special place to meet with God. I want to be just like him. I want to go to the places he goes; I want to see what he sees, and I want the same encounters with this One he loves so much.

Just as I followed in my earthly father's footsteps down that dirt path so many years ago, my Heavenly Father is calling me to follow Him on the roads of life. And perhaps, just as my father's steps were difficult to pursue, there will be times when Jesus' path for me will be challenging to navigate.

Yet we can determine in our hearts to follow Jesus no matter where He may lead. We have the assurance that our Guide is ushering us into the sanctuary where He will meet with us.

King David describes this truth in Psalm 23: the Lord is our good Shepherd who leads us, His sheep. David knows that God ultimately guides us gently onto good paths—paths directing us into His presence and according to His will.

Sweet soul, the road you are walking may be a hard one to navigate. Perhaps the Lord is guiding you into unfamiliar territory. Take heart. Though you may not understand where Jesus is directing, you can trust that there's no circumstance you will experience where He has not already gone before you. The Father is close beside you—and He will meet you right here in the middle of the hardship.

PAUSE:

Read Psalm 23; Proverbs 4:11; John 10:11-18.

PONDER:

Where is Jesus leading me today? Why do I find it difficult to follow? Am I willing to trust that He is guiding me in the right path?

PRAY:

Dear Father, increase my trust in Your good guidance. When I find it difficult to take the next step, let me find my strength in You. Where I struggle, please help me.
In Jesus' name, Amen.

DAY 14
A Light for My Path

Your word is a lamp to my feet
and a light to my path.
(Psalm 119:105)

"I'll call your mama and tell her to turn the outside light on for you," my aunt assured ten-year-old me as I closed her door and started walking from her house back to mine in the darkness. Apprehensively, I placed my bare feet onto the grassy path I was sure led home.

Feeling the thick blades of grass-stubble fold under my toes, I glanced through the shadows cast by the moonlight and dancing in the looming oak trees to calculate each step. This went on for what felt like an eternity, but it was only a few minutes.

Then suddenly, the carport light from my house popped on, flooded the darkness, and illuminated my track home. Now my steps became certain of their direction. I skipped all the way home until I was safely inside and closed the door on the dark behind me.

During the summers of my childhood, a quick visit to my aunt's house next door would often result in my staying until the sun said goodnight. And so, when I had to return home, my course was shrouded by uncertainty and fear—until Mama threw on the outside lamp and the light overshadowed the darkness.

As I've journeyed the road from childhood to adulthood—and on to middle age—many times my way was obscured in nights of trouble and bewilderment. Deciphering the steps to make it safely through difficulties was challenging—and I'm positive more of these times will come. Yet through it all, I could turn to Someone to light my way—the Word of God Himself, Jesus.

When our minds are muddied by fear, Scripture can illuminate the path to faith. As the psalmist says: "Your word is a lamp to my feet and a light to my path" (Ps. 119:105). When our hearts are swallowed by loneliness, despair, and hopelessness, we can rely on the Lord's presence always being with us (Matt. 28:20; Heb. 13:5b).

Where the way ahead is obscured from view and anxiety refuses to loosen its grip, we can hold to Jesus' promise of peace beyond understanding (Phil. 4:7).

Friend, standing on the promises of God's Word dispels darkness and provides a floodlight to guide our hearts to trust Him to lead us in the way. Are you facing a path shrouded in darkness? There's no need to fear because our Father has provided His Word, overflowing with promises to illuminate the way ahead. You only need to trust the Lord—and take Him at His Word.

Pause:

Read Psalm 119:105-112; Hebrews 4:12; Luke 1:79.

Ponder:

In what area of your heart do you need God's light to shine? What Scriptures offer you guidance in the right way?

Pray:

Dear Father, thank you that Your Word brings light in areas of uncertainty. Guide my heart to the truth that dispels the darkness and help me trust Your promises.
In Jesus' name, Amen.

DAY 15
He Guides Me with Love

"He found him in a desert land,
and in the howling waste of the wilderness;
he encircled him, he cared for him,
he kept him as the apple of his eye.
The LORD alone guided him."
(Deuteronomy 32:10, 12a)

Startled awake in the wee hours of the morning, I was twisted in my bed linens and laid in a puddle of sweat. *God has left you here alone.* The lie echoed in my mind.

My resolve to fight the enemy waned. I swiped damp hair from my forehead and turned onto my side—and tried to choke back tears. But it was futile.

I couldn't identify the Lord's hand in my circumstances, feel His presence, or understand His plan. Long years of chronic pain, battles with anxiety and depression, and countless sleepless nights had led me to a desert place.

I imagine the Israelites felt similar walking through the wilderness, year after year with the Promised Land nowhere in sight. Yes, they made poor choices that prolonged their stay. And no, they did not always heed the words of the Lord and suffered the consequences.

While their extended desert-dwelling was their fault, sometimes we walk through wastelands free from blame: we are placed there by our sovereign Lord.

Blessedly, just as the loving hand of the Father stayed upon the Israelites, it is ever upon you and me.

In Deuteronomy, the Israelites' forty years of wilderness wandering was ending. Moses laid down his mantle and Joshua took it up to finish the last leg of the race. But before the people walked into the Promised Land, Moses called them to remember their Father's faithfulness, and how He led them each step of the way.

Moses declared the goodness of the Lord to Israel: "He found him in a desert land, and in the howling waste of the wilderness; he encircled him, he cared for him, he kept him as the apple of his eye. The LORD alone guided him" (Deut. 32:10, 12a). And what God did for His children in Bible times, He will do for you and me today.

Looking back on that morning, Satan whispered a lie that God had forgotten me. But the hand of my Father rested upon me. His strength kept me. When I was tempted to lose all hope, He lifted my floundering heart.

Day-by-day, God sent help through my family who cared for me. Ultimately, He led me out of that particular wilderness season by bringing trusted professionals who came alongside me to rebuild my broken body. And thankfully, my health struggles decreased.

In this life, the Father's way can sometimes feel hidden from us. Rather than turning to despair, you can be certain God knows all the details of your life. He is ever seeing, caring, and guiding His children down the right path. When the enemy whispers lies, shout the truth of your Father's lovingkindness. He will lead you out of the desert places, and keep you in the center of His eye.

PAUSE:

Read Deuteronomy 32:7-14; Nehemiah 9:12; Psalm 32:7-10.

PONDER:

Remember a time you were in a wilderness season. Where can you trace the hand of God leading you out? How does this encourage your heart in the present trial you face?

PRAY:

Dear Father, when trials linger and I'm unable to see Your hand, help me remember that You are with me. Thank You for always guiding me with lovingkindness along the paths of this life. In Jesus' name, Amen.

⇝ DAY 16 ⇜

He Brings Me to a Glorious End

"For the Lamb in the midst of the throne
will be their shepherd,
and he will guide them to springs of living water,
and God will wipe away every tear from their eyes."
(Revelation 7:17)

I maneuvered the gear shift into reverse and slowly backed out of my driveway. I had no idea where I was going. I just hoped a change in scenery would quiet my heart and calm my swirling thoughts—if only for a short time. It had been a tough couple of weeks. My body struggled with fatigue, my mind battled anxiety, and troubles piled high on my heart.

I wheeled my car onto the road and headed toward town. After navigating around the one traffic circle announcing the arrival to city limits, a sign for the local university appeared and I remembered the campus had a lake. So, I quickly adjusted my course, parked my car, and began walking on the path to the waterside.

As I rounded the corner of a campus building, a distant view of the lake materialized. My eyes caught the view of the sun's reflection shimmering on the water's surface and I stopped. The magnificent beauty of—what seemed like—God smiling upon the water was spellbinding.

Unexpectedly, tears of relief bubbled up and spilled down my face. I realized at that moment that not only was God smiling on the lake, but He was smiling on me. The Lord reminded me of His presence—and I was certain that He had led me to this place.

On the hard days of life, I find myself quoting Revelation 7:17: "For the Lamb in the midst of the throne will be their shepherd, and he will guide them to springs of living water, and God will wipe away every tear from their eyes."

This promise reminds us that our Father in heaven is always guiding us—and He will lead us to a glorious end. The place that He is leading us to is free from trouble, heartache, pain, and tears. Our hearts will thirst no more as the Lord fills us with Himself.

Standing by the edge of the lake years ago, I didn't drink its waters to quench my thirst—that would have been futile—nor did my suffering suddenly end. But I praised the Lord for being the source of living water for my thirsty soul.

One day, our Father will dry our tears forever. He's ever guiding us into a place of relief, joy, and peace. Friend, don't ever doubt that He is doing this for you.

Pause:

Read Revelation 7:9-17; Psalm 16:11;
Isaiah 25:8.

Ponder:

How does knowing your Father is leading you to a glorious end to all of your troubles encourage your heart to keep following Him? Take a moment to imagine the day when all your tears will be wiped away, and praise Him!

Pray:

Dear Father, thank You for the promise of an eternity without sorrow, pain, or tears. When this life gets hard, let me remember that You are leading me to a glorious end. Fill me with hope, joy, and peace as I trust You.
In Jesus' name, Amen.

SECTION 5

A TRUSTWORTHY FATHER

DAY 17
When I Need a Shelter

God is our refuge and strength,
a very present help in trouble.
(Psalm 46:1)

Dust from the dirt path leading home bounced around my feet and I sprinted as fast as I could. As a six-year-old, I had been playing with one of the neighborhood kids when a man showed up to visit her family. As he approached the circle of laughter that my friend's and I formed, my mind screamed: "Stranger Danger." In my childlike imagination, I took his nearness as a threat.

Tears pooled around my chin and I struggled to catch my breath as he came closer. After backing away from his presence, I turned my feet toward home and kept running as the words echoed in my mind: *Just get to Daddy and everything will be okay!*

It wasn't long before I burst into the backdoor of our house and found Daddy standing in the kitchen. He took one look at my face and opened his arms to me. I fell into his embrace and spluttered: "That man is going to hurt us!" Immediately, Daddy stood and rushed out to take care of the problem.

I knew Daddy was going to protect me and that in his care, I was safe from danger.

Scriptures are full of examples of those who faced trouble, found themselves staring down an enemy, and were caught in tight places. The Israelites experienced all of these (see Exod. 14-15). Yet the author of Psalm 46 declares that "God is our refuge and strength, a very present help in trouble" (v. 1).

The Hebrew translation for the word "refuge" found in this Scripture is *maḥăsê*, and means "a shelter, a rock of refuge." God is dependable in times of crises—a solid rock and shelter for His people.

Just as I ran to Daddy and knew that He would take care of me, we can trust our Heavenly Father to be our refuge when everything around us is falling apart. Going to our Father is always the right choice—both with our real or imagined fears. He is our shelter, our protection, and our defense—God is a rescuer. And every resource we need can be found in His presence.

Daddy returned into the house to tell me the identity of the man who was visiting our neighbors. He explained that there was never any real danger and promised that I was safe to go about my normal routine—and his words proved true. That man never scared me again.

Sweet soul, there is a promise in this Scripture that you and I can cling to. It is the promise of our Father's trustworthiness in times of trouble. He will be our shelter from harm and give us His presence now and forevermore. Let's hold on to this good news and never let go.

Pause:
Read Psalm 46; Psalm 91:2;
Hebrews 6:18.

Ponder:
What trouble do you face today? Take a moment to envision God as a shelter who you can run to with it. How does His presence with you help you trust Him?

Pray:
Dear Father, sometimes fear overtakes me, and I forget to run to You with it. Help me trust that You are my shelter. Show me Your presence in every situation that I face.
In Jesus' name, Amen.

⇝ DAY 18 ⇜
No Need to Fear

Fear not, for I am with you; be not dismayed,
for I am your God; I will strengthen you,
I will help you, I will uphold you with
my righteous right hand.
(Isaiah 41:10)

The winding road led up the mountainside and darkness enveloped my car. As I climbed higher in elevation, fog wrapped itself around my car and decreased my visibility until I could barely see the road ahead. I scurried to the middle lane to avoid plowing into the guard rail and struggled to stay calm. But fear sunk its hook into my heart.

My breath became shallow and my heart thundered in my throat. With my stomach twisted in knots, a command echoed through my mind: *Breathe, breathe, breathe.* Accepting that no one but the Lord could help me, I whispered a prayer: "Lord, help me get through this safely. Please keep me from panicking."

Although it felt like forever driving in the haze, I was only minutes away from the exit to the retreat center that held my reservation. Once I wheeled my car off the highway and pulled into the parking lot, air filled my lungs and I thanked the Lord for deliverance.

Later that night, snuggled safely in bed, my memory replayed the terrifying events of my trek up the mountain. God's promise in Isaiah 41:10 bubbled to the front of my thoughts: "Fear not, for I am with you; be not dismayed, for I am your God; I will strengthen you, I will help you, I will uphold you with my righteous right hand."

In Isaiah 41, the people of Israel stared at a ruined city overtaken by their enemies. Living in exile, they probably felt like the fog of darkness had enveloped them. God's chosen people struggled to recognize their surroundings and fear likely filled their hearts. Yet God was calling them to continue in the path He had set before them. And though fear within them was great, His promises were greater still.

Within this one Scripture, God provided everything needed to squash fear. He assured the Israelites of His constant presence, mighty power, and help along the way. And the good news is that this promise is ours as well.

We can trade our fears with trust by claiming every word of this promise. Our Father is trustworthy to bring us through obscure and winding circumstances. He has every resource we need to find peace, comfort, and safety.

Perhaps you're traveling on an uphill road and you've been blindsided by unexpected circumstances. Your heart, like mine, may be prone to fear. Take heart, friend. Find rest in His presence. The Father will help you and hold you firmly in His hand. You can trust that God will never let you go.

Pause:

Read Isaiah 41; Psalm 27:1; Romans 8:31.

Ponder:

In what situation are you struggling with fearing what you cannot see? How does applying this promise to your situation help you trust your Father?

Pray:

Dear Father, I struggle with fear when I can't see my way through a situation. Help me remember that Your presence is always with me and Your help is always available. You are my Mighty God. I trust You to walk with me through every circumstance.
In Jesus' name, Amen.

DAY 19

Trusting the Father When I Don't Understand

Trust in the LORD *with all your heart,*
and do not lean on your own understanding.
In all your ways acknowledge him,
and he will make straight your paths.
(Proverbs 3:5-6)

The tune of *'Tis So Sweet to Trust in Jesus* plays softly in the background as I sit to tackle the day's tasks before me. Deadlines loom, messages piling in my inbox scream for my attention, and a list of personal needs must be addressed. But the song catches my attention and its familiar lyrics slip easily from my tongue.

Tis so sweet to trust in Jesus,
Just to take him at his word;
Just to rest upon His promise;
Just to know, "Thus saith the Lord."

I'm ushered into a holy moment—and I don't want to miss it. The Lord prompts me to answer this question: *Do I—and can I—trust Jesus?* Memories flood my mind. All the hard trials that I didn't—and still don't fully—understand. My father's debilitating health that began during my teenage years and eventually led to medication dependency. It wrecked our family. My chronic illness diagnosis at age twenty-six and all the dreams shattered by the years I suffered with it. Times of financial upheaval and anxiety about the future—the list could go on. I bet yours could, too.

Then I recall verses I memorized as a youth: "Trust in the Lord with all your heart, and do not lean on your own understanding. In all your ways acknowledge him, and he will make straight your paths" (Prov. 3:5-6).

And so, I search for a deeper understanding of this text. The word "trust" in the Hebrew translation is *batah*. It means to have confidence in—or reliance on—what is secure. I find no confidence in myself and understand I cannot rely on what I see, feel, or touch in this life. My security can—and will—only come from a deep leaning on my Father rather than my own understanding.

Looking back over all the struggles I've endured in my life, the hand of God led me in safety each step along the way. How do we know the Lord can be trusted? He has proven it time and time again—and He will continue to deliver what He promises.

The Father will do the same for you. He keeps His promises by giving His presence—and guidance—along the bumpy, curvy paths of life. Dear one, let's not lean on our own understanding. Its imperfection is flawed and will fail us. But God's way is perfect and flawless. And while we may not fully grasp His ways, we can rely on Him for safety and security. Hold on to this good news!

PAUSE:

Read Proverbs 3:1-8; Jeremiah 17:7; Ephesians 1:12.

PONDER:

What situation in life leads you to question the trustworthy nature of God? How does an awareness of God's faithfulness and character help you maintain trust in Him?

PRAY:

Dear Father, thank You for being trustworthy in all Your ways. When I don't understand what's going on around me, help me to rely on—and trust in—Your infinite wisdom. I am secure in You. In Jesus' name, Amen.

DAY 20
Trusting the Potter's Hand

The vessel he was making of clay was spoiled
in the potter's hand, and he reworked it
into another vessel, as it seemed good to the potter to do.
"Behold, like the clay in the potter's hand,
so are you in my hand."
(Jeremiah 18:4, 6b)

As I stepped inside my first pottery class, nervous excitement filled me. I found my place behind a table smeared with dried sand. My instructor placed a bag of tools in front of me and explained what each one would be used for. Then she pointed to my assigned pottery wheel to get started.

Grabbing a ball of misshapen clay, I slammed it onto the middle of the wheel to secure it in place before molding. Satisfied it would stay, I cupped the clay in my moistened hands and slowly pressed my foot down on the pedal. As the clay turned effortlessly in my hands, I noticed applying too much pressure made dents in unwanted places. And not enough force meant no progress was made to shape the clay into anything recognizable—or useful. But just the right amount of pressure created exactly what I envisioned—a bowl, plate, or ring-holder. Each item, although not perfect, made precious gifts for my family.

In Jeremiah 18, God described Himself as the Potter and His people as the clay: "Behold, like the clay in the potter's hand, so are you in my hand" (v. 6b). As I formed clay into something beautiful, I thought of the many times I've been lovingly thrown onto the wheel of adversity in order for the Master to mold me into a vessel to honor, glorify, and reflect the Creator.

Sometimes, my situations were difficult surfaces to adhere to—chronic illness, job loss, and relational struggles—to name a few. And the force was so intense I questioned if the Lord still had His hand on me. But in these difficulties, the Father proved Himself trustworthy. He never once took His hand off my life—and He knows exactly how much friction and where to apply it to accomplish His purposes in my life.

Friend, sometimes life throws us onto the wheel of affliction and the pain is overwhelming. In these times, we can be certain our Father uses every situation to mold us into lovely vessels for His glory. As we reside in the Potter's hand, every pain will be exchanged for a magnificent purpose. We can trust Him now and forevermore.

Pause:
Read Jeremiah 18:1-8; Isaiah 64:8;
Romans 8:28.

Ponder:
How can seeing our Father as your Potter help you believe God is making something beautiful out of your painful situations? Make a list of the times God brought blessings out of your hard circumstances.

Pray:
Dear Father, help me trust that even in the most difficult circumstances,
Your hand is upon me. And You are creating something meaningful and good out of the most challenging seasons. Thank You for being my trustworthy Father.
In Jesus' name, Amen.

SECTION 6

A PROVIDING FATHER

↠ DAY 21 ↞
Unexpected Gifts of Goodness

Now to him who is able to do far more abundantly than all that we ask or think, according to the power at work within us.
(Ephesians 3:20)

Thumbing through the catalog, my eyes lit up when I saw the shiny gold ring. My birthstone—a garnet—sat in the middle, enhanced by rose and bronze-colored accents. It was beautiful, and if I could ever get one, it was exactly what I'd want.

But I quickly closed the pages of the book and stored it under my bed. I had resigned myself to the fact that, while all my high school classmates ordered class rings to commemorate graduation, I would go without one. After months of battling constant migraine headaches that led to chronic illness, my daddy's sickness had cost him his job as a pastor—our family's primary source of income. And so, asking my parents for something so exorbitant was out of the question; it was all they could do to provide our necessities.

But I had no idea that God was working behind the scenes.

It was only a few days later when a couple from the church my dad had pastored arrived to visit our family. Cornering me in the kitchen, the sweet lady placed her hand on my shoulder and smiled as she shared the unexpected news. "I know that it's time to order your class ring and I want you to pick out the exact one you want. It doesn't matter the cost because some of the couples from church are pulling together to pay for it. We love your father—and you. This is our gift to you."

I tried to turn her down graciously, but she wouldn't hear of it. Finally, I gave up and swallowed down grateful tears as I eked out a quiet "Thank you."

In Paul's letter to the Ephesians, he makes a beautiful declaration: "Now to him who is able to do far more abundantly than all that we ask or think, according to the power at work within us, to him be glory in the church and in Christ Jesus throughout all generations, forever and ever. Amen" (Eph. 3:20-21).

Admittedly, this is one of my favorite Scriptures. It brings calm to my heart, peace to my soul, and joy to my spirit to stand on the truth that it reveals: *He is able!* These three words encompass every need that we may experience in this whole wide world—and as long as we shall live.

And not only is God "able," He is more than able—able to do far more abundantly than all that we ask or think. This verse should cause us to stand in awe of our Father's power—and His promise—to go far beyond what we could ever comprehend, envision, or expect.

As I walked across the stage at my graduation, it was with a beautiful class ring on my hand that I never expected to be able to wear. Even today, many years later, that ring points to God's kindness and provision in my life—and acts as a symbol of His ability to do more than I ever expect!

Certainly, we are not promised class rings, designer goods, or every wish that arises in our lives. But we are promised God's provision for each need that we do have, and because of His great love for us, He even surprises us with special gifts. All glory to our great Father!

PAUSE:

Read Ephesians 3:20-21; 2 Chronicles 25:9; 2 Corinthians 9:8.

PONDER:

What need comes to your mind right now? How does knowing that Your Father is able to go above and beyond that need bring joy to Your heart?

PRAY:

Dear Father, as I come to You with my needs, help me to believe that You are able to answer above what I could ask or think. Thank You for the ways You've already provided for me throughout my life. I praise You for being my Great Provider.
In Jesus' name, Amen.

DAY 22
He Provides Himself

Jesus said to her, "Everyone who drinks
of this water will be thirsty again,
but whoever drinks of the water that I will give him
will never be thirsty again.
The water that I will give him will become in him
a spring of water welling up to eternal life."
(John 4:13-14)

On the hot summer days of my childhood, I played outside. I often took breaks to run barefoot across the grassy path leading to our paved driveway. Warmed by the sun's heat, the asphalt scorched my toes as I raced up the front porch steps, swung the door open, and made my way to the kitchen faucet.

As I twisted the faucet, the cold well-water gushed out. I held my cup underneath it until it overflowed, then raised it to my dry lips. *Gulp, Gulp, Gulp.* I drained the water from the glass so fast I lost my breath.

Nothing compares to quenching our thirst when our throats are parched and dry. And we experience the same thirst in our souls when difficulties bear down on our hearts.

In John 4, Jesus is sitting by a well in Samaria when a woman approaches to draw water. All knowing, Jesus recognizes this woman's thirst for more than physical water—her soul is also parched. She's an outcast with five past marriages and now lives with a man who is not her husband (John 4:17-18). The Samaritan woman doesn't need water from a well dug into the dirt of this earth, but something more lasting. And it's the same water each of our hearts need in this life.

This water—the living water of Jesus—has the power to transform our hearts from the inside out and deliver us to eternity.

And the good news is that Jesus offers eternal water freely to us just as He offered it to the Samaritan woman—and only He can provide it. Jesus said to her, "Everyone who drinks of this water will be thirsty again, but whoever drinks of the water that I will give him will never be thirsty again. The water that I will give him will become in him a spring of water welling up to eternal life" (John 4:13-14).

Sister, since we are daughters of God, we know that Jesus quenches the thirst of our parched souls. He is the source of living water—and everything we need. Jesus offers living water as an invitation to a lasting relationship with Him, the One who can supply all our needs now and forever.

When our hearts are thirsty for joy, comfort, hope, peace, companionship, or love, we can find it in Jesus. These needs can only be satisfied by—and through—Him. All we have to do is ask. Hallelujah!

PAUSE:

Read John 4:1-45; Jeremiah 31:25;
John 7:37-39.

PONDER:

What does your heart thirst for today? Make a list and ask Jesus to fill it with His living water that never runs dry.

PRAY:

Dear Father, I have deep needs only You can meet. Help me trust You to supply them as my heart thirsts for more of You. Thank You for providing living water to quench the longings of my soul.
In Jesus' name, Amen.

⇝ DAY 23 ⇜
The Help I Need

I lift up my eyes to the hills.
From where does my help come?
My help comes from the L*ORD*,
who made heaven and earth.
(Psalm 121:1-2)

"Miss Strickland, I need help!" I must've heard this a thousand times in the few years I served as an elementary school teacher. My students yelled it out for a wide range of needs, from something as small as a pencil lead snapping in two to requesting intervention when an argument needed to be settled.

After hearing a child's cry of desperation, I quickly replied, "It's okay. There's nothing we can't handle." And in the classroom, there wasn't anything I couldn't tackle. I'd swiftly solve the problem—sometimes by coming alongside the child with instructions—and calm replaced the chaos within our four walls.

Yet sometimes in my life, I couldn't manage the problem—long years of chronic illness, financial upheaval, relational struggles due to my father's dependency on medication, and the list could go on.

Like my students, when I stood facing what felt like a mountain to climb, I found myself calling out for the Lord's help.

During those difficult seasons, the psalmist's words in Psalm 121:1-2 focused my heart on my Helper: "I lift up my eyes to the hills. From where does my help come? My help comes from the LORD, who made heaven and earth." Psalm 121 was written while the Israelites were on a pilgrimage. It is a Psalm of Ascent likely sung by God's people as they traveled up the mountainside to Jerusalem.

Perhaps the writer penned these words while surveying the mountain before him knowing God's presence was already there. Maybe his heart leaped with praise and expectation for the joy awaiting him upon his arrival to the top—the place he could worship the Lord.

Or perhaps his heart was anxious as he considered all the resources needed for the journey to be a successful one—resources he couldn't supply himself. Either way, the psalmist focused his eyes and his heart on the Lord, knowing whatever provision was required for the journey to be successful, God would deliver it to His children.

Friend, we are certain to face mountains and need help along life's journey. But we don't face them alone. Like the psalmist, we can sing of our Father's provision because He "will neither slumber nor sleep" (v. 4b). Surely, we can call on our Father for help and—with hopeful expectation—we can offer our praise for His provision for exactly what is required to make it to the end of our journey.

Pause:
Read Psalm 121; Psalm 91; Proverbs 3:5-6.

Ponder:
What problem are you facing today
that you need help solving?
How can crying out to God for help bring
calm while you allow Him to work it out?

Pray:
Dear Father, when challenges overwhelm
my heart, remind me to cry out to You.
I trust You're my one True Helper.
Thank You for being a Father who can solve
any dilemma and provide for my every need.
I give You praise and glory forever.
In Jesus' name, Amen.

DAY 24
An Answer for Worry

"Look at the birds of the air: they neither sow nor reap
nor gather into barns,
and yet your heavenly Father feeds them.
Are you not of more value than they?
And which of you by being
anxious can add a single hour to his span of life?"
(Matthew 6:26-27)

When my husband's change in career took him back to school as a full-time student, our main source of income was gone for a few years. After his program's completion, being an older graduate seeking employment brought slammed doors to new opportunities. No matter how hard he knocked, nothing seemed to open.

Desperation and anxiety crept in during those nights. I lay awake wondering how we were going to make it—and prayed for God to swing open a door. Morning would come and I'd busy myself with mundane tasks to avoid thinking about what could happen if nothing changed. Over and over, I was caught in this loop.

Until early one morning, I was startled awake by a bird chirping in the tree outside my window. The sun was still hiding outside and darkness filled the sky. Yet the bird's song rose in beauty. It drawled out the lows and climbed through the highs of its melody. What could it be singing about at such an early hour?

Matthew 6:26-27 echoed in my mind: "Look at the birds of the air; they do not sow or reap or store away in barns, and yet your heavenly Father feeds them. Are you not much more valuable than they? Can any one of you by worrying add a single hour to your life?"

That's when I knew the Lord was speaking to me. He used that little bird's song of trust to quiet my heart and calm my anxious mind. I imagined the bird was singing in expectation of the sun's appearance. Perhaps this tiny creature was resting in the promise that the sun would surely rise and the Creator would meet each need the day presented.

Then I recalled my blessings. All my life, I had never come to the table and not had food to eat. Never experienced a lack of clothing. Nor had I gone without necessities. Assuredly, if my Father had done it before, He would do it again. And so, I chose to trade my worries for rest, relying on His promise to care for me.

What worries are circling your mind? Maybe you're wondering how you will face the day before you. Let's take a lesson from the birds and trust our loving Father will provide all we need to make it through the day. After all, He has promised to care—and provide—for each of our needs.

Pause:

Read Matthew 6:26-34; Philippians 4:19; 1 Peter 5:7.

Ponder:

How does knowing your Father cares for the birds—lowly creatures—reveal His great love for you?
List circumstances in your life you can release into God's care. Ask the Lord to help you trust Him to provide your every need.

Pray:

Dear Father, sometimes it's difficult to trust You when I am consumed with worries. Help me believe in Your promise to provide all I need. Thank You for caring for me. In Jesus' name, Amen.

SECTION 7

A PROTECTING FATHER

DAY 25
Safe in His Care

He said to them, "Why are you afraid, O you of little faith?" Then he rose and rebuked the winds and the sea, and there was a great calm.
(Matthew 8:26)

The smell of the salty air filled my nose as I held tightly to the metal edge of our small boat. The violent rocking produced terror in my ten-year-old heart as waves from the passing yacht pounded our unworthy sea vessel. Water ricocheted everywhere.

Daddy sat at the back of the boat steering us out of the path of the choppy wake. As the tears spilled onto my cheeks and a scream welled up inside, I immediately caught sight of my daddy. His eyes connected with mine and his assurance was immediate: "It's okay, Rosann. Everything is okay."

Daddy had purchased our boat when it was bare-boned. He and my brother worked tirelessly to repair, reform, and redesign it along with totally overhauling the motor. And because of his work, he knew something that my fearful heart didn't know—he knew what the boat was capable of, and how to steer it out of the path of the violent waves to safety. I only had to trust him.

Perhaps this is a little like how the disciples felt when crossing the Sea of Galilee during an unexpected storm (Matt. 8:23-37). Waves shook their boat and fear assailed them, yet Jesus slept. When they woke Him and screamed to be saved, He wondered why they were so concerned. After all, the Father was still in control. He alone was the Creator of the winds and the seas. And so when Christ spoke, the winds ceased. Calm replaced the chaos.

The storms of life are inevitable—we cannot escape them. But when we find ourselves shaken by the uncertainties, we can look first to our Father—the Master of the wind and the seas—instead of focusing on the tumultuous waves of our circumstances. Praise the Lord, we do not have to fear when our Father is near!

PAUSE:

Read Matthew 8:23-27; John 14:27;
2 Timothy 1:7.

PONDER:

Name any areas in your life where you doubt God's control. How have you allowed the waves to fill you with fear? Take time to imagine Jesus speaking to your storm and allow Him to replace your fear with peace.

PRAY:

Dear Father, thank You for being a God who speaks peace to the storm. Forgive me for the times I doubt Your power and succumb to fear. Renew my faith in You, and calm the storms that surround me.
In Jesus' name, Amen.

DAY 26

He Surrounds What's Surrounding Me

"Do not be afraid, for those who are with us are more than those who are with them."
(2 Kings 6:16)

I don't like traveling alone at night, especially along an unfamiliar route. One night, with my ears tuned to the voice of my Google maps guide, I slowed, stopped, and turned for what seemed like an eternity onto roads I hoped were taking me home. I was navigating two hours home from my mother's new house in the dark for the first time. Visiting there during daylight was fine, but driving back at night, I willed my hands to release their tight grip on the steering wheel. I concentrated on deep breathing—and prayed for the Lord's protection on the highway.

Finally, I rolled into the parking space at home and familiar headlights illuminated my car's cabin. A grin split my husband's face as he exited his car beside me. "I tracked your location and got behind you to follow you home." A deep breath exited my lungs. I had expected him to stay another night in our hometown, but he had been with me all along.

When we travel down dark and unfamiliar paths in life, it's easy to get caught in battles of fear—and think we're completely alone. The enemy tries to convince us we'll be overtaken, defeated, and abandoned.

Perhaps this is the same way Elisha's servant felt when he was surrounded by enemies in 2 Kings 6. The evil king of Aram ordered his army to capture the prophet Elisha and his servant because every wicked plan the king made against Israel, God revealed to Elisha. This inside intel kept the Israelites from his trap. So, the king ordered an army to encompass the city where Elisha and his servant were staying. When Elisha's servant saw the vast army, he asked: "Alas, my master! What shall we do?" (v. 15b).

But Elisha's faith was steadfast. He told his servant, "Do not be afraid, for those who are with us are more than those who are with them." Then Elisha prayed and said, "O Lord, please open his eyes that he may see." So the Lord opened the eyes of the young man, and he saw, and behold, the mountain was full of horses and chariots of fire all around Elisha (vv. 16-17).

The good news is—as children of God—we never fight our battles alone. Warfare will come in this life brought on by sickness, relational discord, rejection, financial upheaval, or fill in the blank. We won't know what to do—or have control.

Our human eyes may be tempted to focus on the army circling us and let fear and despair rise, but we are assured that all of heaven is on our side. Our Father surrounds what surrounds us—and His presence is with us always. Take heart, sweet sister: your Father has already won the war!

Pause:
Read 2 Kings 6:8-23; Psalm 34:4-7; Psalm 91:11.

Ponder:
What battle of darkness envelops you today? How does knowing—even if you may not see it—that Your Father surrounds you with His presence and offers you protection bring hope to your heart?

Pray:
Dear Father, when battles of darkness and fear threaten to overwhelm me, help me look to You instead of my circumstances. Remind me I am never alone and that You are always in control. Thank You for surrounding me with Your protection. In Jesus' name, Amen.

DAY 27
My Hope of Deliverance

He delivered us from such a deadly peril,
and he will deliver us.
On him we have set our hope that
he will deliver us again.
(2 Corinthians 1:10)

As I swept the tiled floor of my kitchen, my mind ruminated over all the things going wrong in my life. Still struggling with bouts of chronic illness—check. Financial upheaval—check. My parent's recent separation without a move toward reunification—check. My father's substance abuse with no signs of recovery—check.

On and on I mentally listed the struggles seeming to increase daily. To say the battle in my heart was intense would've been an understatement. I prayed for God's rescue while I carried out the most mundane tasks. "Lord, I don't know what You're doing, but could You do it fast? I don't think I can handle this much longer." I whispered.

While I gathered dust into a pile on the floor, my heart felt scattered in the wind, and I was tempted to give up hope of God ever delivering me from the perils encircling me. But I know God's hand of protection was on my life. And although I won't attempt to compare my sufferings with the Apostle Paul's, during that year—and the years that proceeded—when never-ending trials piled on, I found great hope in Paul's writings.

In 2 Corinthians 1:10, Paul gave glory to God despite his hardships, and declared: "He delivered us from such a deadly peril, and he will deliver us. On him we have set our hope that he will deliver us again."

If anyone could compile a dossier on God's protection, Paul is the best choice. He experienced it over and over again. I imagine Paul checking his own boxes of troubles: shipwrecked three times, beaten, imprisoned, lost at sea, weary, in pain, falsely accused, hungry, thirsty—and various other afflictions (2 Cor. 11:2–12:21). But God delivered him out of them all—and Paul, with his heart filled with hope, trusted His Father for deliverance for whatever trials the future held.

And like Paul, we can hold on to the hope of God's deliverance from *all* our trials. Assuredly, our Father in Heaven will deliver us safely through every trying season. You—and I—can trust that God will protect us in every hardship, even if our deliverance is not completed until we reach the other side.

PAUSE:

Read 2 Corinthians 9-10;
2 Corinthians 11:21–12:21; 2 Peter 2:9.

PONDER:

What is on the list of trials facing you? How does knowing Your Father will protect and deliver you, help your heart hope in Him?

PRAY:

Dear Father, when I face battles of pain, fear, and trouble, let me remember You are my protection, deliverance, and hope to the end. Thank You for keeping me safe now and evermore. In Jesus' name, Amen.

➻ DAY 28 ➻
Covered by Him

For he will hide me in his shelter in the day of trouble;
he will conceal me under the cover of his tent;
he will lift me high upon a rock.
(Psalm 27:5)

I struggled to swallow the lump in my throat and I willed my heart to slow its thumping. My terrier's wide eyes matched the fear pouring into my body. The thunderous rain outside my window covered my home in darkness and the winds let out a deafening tone. I stole a glance at my husband sitting beside me. If he wasn't panicking, maybe I shouldn't either.

"Should we take cover in the hallway?" My voice quavered as the question tumbled from my mouth. His eyes darted to survey our outside surroundings. Already rising, he replied, "Yes!"

While I jolted to my feet to follow him, I grabbed our terrier and took a few steps before sliding my body down the wall of our narrow hallway. I had never heard such howling sounds before, so I quietly prayed for God to keep us safe until the tornado passed by.

As I sat knee to knee with my husband, I saw our pup do something that mirrored what I was experiencing inside my own fearful heart. The dog scooted up against my spouse and used her nose to wedge a hole under his armpit until her entire head was covered with his arm. Our terrier had sought shelter and security in her master's covering during life's calamities—and my heart longs to do the same.

In Psalm 27, King David was caught in a life-threatening situation. He was being chased by the jealous and murderous King Saul who had placed a bounty on his head. Perhaps the winds of his heart howled like the winds surrounding my home on that day we bunkered down in the hallway.

But despite this dangerous situation, David remained confident of His Father's care—and reminded himself where to turn when everything around him was crashing down: "For he will hide me in his shelter in the day of trouble; he will conceal me under the cover of his tent; he will lift me high upon a rock" (Ps. 27:5).

The good news is that we can have the same confidence King David had. In times of trouble—whether literal or figurative storms—we can run into the arms of our Father for shelter and trust He will cover us with Himself. He provides the love, peace, and hope we need to endure the trials of this life—and His grace will lead us safely to our heavenly home.

Thankfully, the tornado left only scattered debris, broken tree limbs, and some missing roof shingles. But I also learned an important lesson from our dog—the safest place to be in rain or shine is the shelter of our Master. He is our hiding place. Hallelujah!

Pause:

Read Psalm 27; Psalm 57:1; Matthew 7:25.

Ponder:

When the storms of trouble roll into your life, where do you run to for help? How does knowing your Father will shelter you during the storms help your heart not to fear?

Pray:

Dear Father, help me run into Your presence for shelter during the hard times of this life. I trust You to be my hiding place. Thank You for protection now—and forever more.
In Jesus' name, Amen.

SECTION 8

A COMFORTING FATHER

↠ DAY 29 ↞

Favor in Every Situation

His favor is for a lifetime. Weeping may tarry for the night, but joy comes with the morning.
(Psalm 30:5)

Years ago, after moving to a new city, I struggled deeply with all of the changes I was facing.

Regardless of whether we've moved or not, all of us know what it's like to walk through new seasons that are difficult—seasons consisting of new diagnoses, a new title (i.e., divorcee, widow), or new griefs. These changes can leave us feeling depleted, out of favor, far from home, or without support to fall back on.

I remember feeling this way in that new city, and so I scheduled a meeting with my new pastor. I shook his hand with sweaty palms, and he motioned for me to sit. In our conversation, I mentioned that my father had been a past student at the Bible College where the Pastor had once taught.

I was happy to claim my dad when he asked for his name, and the pastor smiled immediately, "Oh, I remember him. A good man."

Our visit ended with a promise. "Anything you need, day or night, I'm only a phone call away. Because I know your father, I will be a father to you also." Although this pastor barely knew me, he showed me favor—simply because of who my father was.

That connection with my new pastor offered me some footing in an unstable season. And it also pointed out this biblical truth: "His favor is for a lifetime. Weeping may tarry for the night, but joy comes with the morning" (Ps. 30:5).

Although I was in a "night" season of sorrow and struggle in that new city, there was still favor on my life—because God was my Father. And lately, as I have found myself struggling again in a new season full of incredible pain, heartache, and difficulty, the Word has reminded me of God's continued favor on my life.

It's not because I have earned that favor; I simply have His favor because I am His child.

Focus on that for a moment—God's favor, in Christ, endures for a lifetime for those who belong to Him! He provides joy each morning. And although there may continue to be tears, He gives His children the ultimate security of eternity with Himself, when "He will wipe away every tear" (Rev. 21:4).

Assuredly, God goes before us, stays with us, and is with us no matter where life leads. He promises favor to His children. We can trust Him to wipe away our tears, comfort our sorrows, and lead us along dark paths into marvelous light.

PAUSE:

Read Psalm 30:5; Psalm 84:11; Revelation 21:4.

PONDER:

How can you focus on God's favor in your current situation? List some ways that you can trust that He will bring joy through the heartache—if not now, eventually.

PRAY:

Dear Father, as I walk in this season, help me remember that I am Your beloved daughter. Help me understand that because I am Your child, I can trust that Your favor shines over me even when I feel like I am walking alone. In Jesus' name, Amen.

⤞ DAY 30 ⤝

Help in Loneliness

So she called the name of the Lord who spoke to her,
"You are a God of seeing," for she said,
"Truly here I have seen him who looks after me."
(Genesis 16:13)

Instead of the place I envisioned, I found loneliness.

Sitting in my freshman dorm room, the burlap-covered walls closed in on me. I curled into a ball as tears pooled onto the pink flowers adorning the blanket my mother helped me pick out before we made the two-hour drive to my college campus—my home for the next four years.

It was the first time I'd been away from home for an extended time. The one hundred miles separating me from family, lifelong friends, and all that was familiar seemed a continent away.

Each day, I walked in a sea of people who didn't know my name, speak with the same small-town dialect, or share my life experiences as a Native American. And after the new wore off, assignments piled up, and only surface-level friendships remained, my heart ached for the comforts of home—where I was certain I would never be alone.

Loneliness hounded me on other occasions, as well. It tormented me in isolation brought on by chronic illness, broken relationships, and bouts of depression. You may be familiar with this agony, too. Hagar faced this emptiness in Genesis 16.

Hagar was in a desolate place after she fled the servanthood of Sarah. Harsh conditions developed within the household after Sarah, Abraham's wife, devised a plan for a child. God had promised heirs to Abraham and Sarah, but He didn't work fast enough for Sarah. She took matters into her own hands and gave her servant, Hagar, to Abraham in hopes that she would produce the child.

When Hagar's pregnancy came to light, Sarah's jealousy ensued. The two women couldn't remain under the same roof, so Hagar fled (Gen. 16:1-6).

Hagar found herself alone in the wilderness. I imagine she felt unknown, unheard, and overlooked. But God saw her and assured her of His presence, purpose, and plan for her life—and the life of her child (Gen. 16:7-12).

Genesis 16:13 records Hagar's response: "So she called the name of the LORD who spoke to her, 'You are a God of seeing,' for she said, 'Truly here I have seen him who looks after me.'"

Hagar calls God, *El Roi*. The Hebrew meaning for "The God Who Sees Me." It's the first name given to God in Scripture—one we can cling to when we are in our deep, dark, and deserted places.

With the Lord's help, I remained at the same college until graduation. I forged friendships, developed life skills, and prepared for a future in the workforce. But most of all, I gained an understanding that the Lord longs to fill the empty places—mainly with Himself. And He wants to do the same for you.

Sweet soul, your Father's eyes are set on you. In the desolate places of your heart, the Lord is with you. Be comforted by this truth: El Roi has His gaze turned toward you. He loves, hears, and cares for you always.

PAUSE:
Read Genesis 16; Psalm 34:16;
Psalm 139:7-10.

PONDER:
What area of your life brings loneliness?
How does knowing El Roi is with you
comfort your heart?

PRAY:
Dear Father, thank You for keeping Your
loving eye upon me. When I struggle with
loneliness, help me remember You
are with me. Your presence provides the
comfort I need. In Jesus' name, Amen.

DAY 31
Never Alone

"I will not leave you orphans; I will come to you."
(John 14:18)

I awoke early to the sound of paws scratching the cotton sheets covering my mattress. With a deep sigh, I rolled onto the opposite side of the bed and ignored my terrier's plea for a walk. With prolonged days of chronic pain, I coveted the times when sleep was available because it provided an escape from constant suffering. But the noise only intensified.

Using every ounce of strength I had, I got up, dressed, and escorted my pup out the door. As my feet sunk into the grass along the well-worn path I took daily with my furry companion, despair threatened to consume me.

After finishing our route, I guided my dog inside and watched her curl up on the edge of the couch, which gave her a pristine view of the wildlife outside. Then I trekked down another familiar path along the narrow hallway of my home leading to my bedroom—the place where I often spent time in prayer.

I dropped to my knees beside the bed and rested my forehead against the leather Bible I gripped tightly in my hands. I petitioned God for comfort as I recounted the painful losses of my life—broken dreams, unmet expectations, a disabled body—and (what felt like) a lack of purpose from all the years of chronic illness.

I begged the Lord to speak peace to my heart as hot tears formed puddles on my Bible's edge—to remove my ashes for His beauty. And just when I felt like my heart would explode, a gentle brush of fur touched my arm as the warm body of my puppy curled up against my thigh. Then a gentle whisper caressed my heart: You're not alone.

The Holy Spirit was reminding me that—as my furry companion nestled up beside me—the Lord's presence was there extending comfort, hope, and peace despite the pain enveloping my heart. And our Father offers the same to each of His children.

In John 14, Jesus spoke to the disciples before His impending death. The One whom they'd sunk all their hopes into was leaving. Grief, disillusionment, and sorrow were sure to follow. Yet Jesus offered a promise that, although He was going away, He would "not leave [them] as orphans," but would send them a "Helper, the Holy Spirit" to dwell with them (v. 18, 26).

John used the Greek word *paraklētos* to define the "Helper" who would come after Jesus ascended to heaven. *Paraklētos* also means "called to one's side, aider, or an advocate." And the KJV Bible uses the word "Comforter" in its place.

Jesus tells the disciples this "Helper, the Holy Spirit" will come alongside to comfort and give them divine strength to endure trials, hardship, and persecutions.

And we have access to the same Holy Spirit that Jesus promised to the disciples. The Holy Spirit is right beside us, helping, guiding, encouraging, and comforting us in every loss we endure.

Dear friend, what grief weighs heavy on your heart? Trust that your Father's presence is with you. He has promised to "never leave you nor forsake you" (Heb. 13:5b). Let this truth comfort your heart.

Pause:

Read John 14:9-31; Matthew 28:20; 2 Corinthians 1:3-4.

Ponder:

What circumstance in your life brings grief to your heart? How does knowing you have a Helper beside you bring comfort to your soul?

Pray:

Dear Father, thank You for being my Comforter. When my heart is downcast, help me remember You are always beside me. Fill my heart with hope, joy, and peace as You give me strength to walk through the pain. In Jesus' name, Amen.

DAY 32
Giving My Concerns to Him

"Cast your burden on the LORD, and he will sustain you; he will never permit the righteous to be moved."
(Psalm 55:22)

I have a pint-sized jar filled with burdens too heavy for me to carry.

Torn shreds of paper rolled into tiny balls hold thin lettered lines defining needs that are impossible for me to meet—a name with the word "salvation" written beside it, emotional healing for a loved one, deliverance from addiction for a friend, comfort for a family who unexpectedly lost a member, and countless other urgencies. These are things that I give to God daily.

The idea for a prayer jar was developed a few years ago while I named my requests one by one on my knees to God. As usual, I was overtaken by overwhelming feelings. I knew the Lord had instructed me to pray—to bring all my requests to Him—but I found myself rising from my prayer time feeling heavier instead of lighter. As I recited each plea, it felt like stacking bricks one atop another onto my own shoulders—and I was crumbling under the weight.

"God, why do I feel worse after prayer?" I whispered, lifting my eyes to heaven. Gently, the Spirit replied: "Cast your burden on the LORD, and he will sustain you" (Ps. 55:22a).

In the original Hebrew, the word cast in this verse is *šālaḵ*. It means "to throw, cast, throw away, cast off, or shed." The psalmist's words implored me to throw my concerns onto Jesus and shed the weight I had mistakenly made my load to carry and my problems to solve.

Looking at the enormity of the situations that needed intervention had placed a boulder on my heart that I was unable to lift. I knew my only choice was to trust in God's sovereignty and release these concerns into His capable hands. *But what would that look like practically?*

When I envisioned flinging these uncertainties onto my Father, I knew since "to cast" is a verb it would involve action. That's when I pulled a mason jar from my kitchen cabinet, started shredding pieces of paper, and began writing the heaviest burdens my heart carried. I rolled each one into a ball and actively tossed it into the container.

The overwhelm I felt moments before was quickly replaced by a sense of relief—relief in knowing that my Heavenly Father's shoulders are big enough to carry my deepest desires, and He can meet every need in my life—and the lives of others (Phil. 4:19).

Since the day I created the prayer jar, I've continued to add deep longings of my heart and the petitions of others who've entrusted me with the loads they carry. Sometimes, I visit the jar and find pleas that have been answered—and I praise God. Yet I'm still waiting for some answers—and I thank God for His sustaining power.

Friend, are you weighed down with concerns today? Creating a prayer jar is not a necessary step to giving your burdens to the Lord. The important thing is to know that your Father invites you to give your burdens to Him. What concerns you, concerns Him. Simply, cast your cares on Him and accept the comfort only He gives.

PAUSE:

Read Psalm 55; Matthew 6:33; 1 Peter 5:7.

PONDER:

Write down the circumstances pressing on your heart. Imagine rolling those burdens onto the shoulders of Jesus knowing He is able to carry them. Accept the comfort this truth gives.

PRAY:

Dear Father, when situations are out of my control, I often feel weighed down. Please help me give these burdens to you and trust You to work them out. Thank You for inviting me to give my concerns to You. In Jesus' name, Amen.

SECTION 9

A HEALING FATHER

↠ DAY 33 ↞
Carried to Jesus

But that you may know that the Son of Man
has authority on earth to forgive sins—
he said to the man who was paralyzed—
"I say to you, rise, pick up your bed and go home."
And immediately he rose up before them and picked up
what he had been lying on and went home, glorifying God.
(Luke 5:24-25)

Beads of perspiration gathered around my brow and I struggled to meet Daddy's worried gaze from my bed. I heard him whisper to my mother, "It's time to take her to the doctor."

Scooping me in his arms, he gently wrapped me in a blanket and leaned me against his side as he supported me to the car.

The drive was an hour to the hospital—and the memory of that long ride is etched forever in my mind. Each shallow breath squeezed my chest and the pain intensified by the minute.

My childhood was plagued by episodes of asthmatic bronchitis, and when I was thirteen years old, it morphed into pneumonia. Mama's medicine cabinet was no match for it that time. That's when I found myself in an emergency room stinging from needles filled with antibiotics and oozing an IV drip. The experience was scary and uncomfortable but it did bring healing to my body.

In the Gospels, we find Jesus performing miracles of healing, and one of those healings occurred for an unnamed man who was paralyzed. This suffering soul was unable to reach Jesus for himself, and so his friends—refusing to be barred by the crowds—lowered the paralytic man down through the roof-top of the building Jesus occupied (Luke 5:17-18).

The determination these friends displayed was not lost on Jesus. He rewarded their faith by healing this man's body—and his soul. Luke records this miracle—and Jesus' ultimate purpose—beautifully: "But that you may know that the Son of Man has authority on earth to forgive sins—he said to the man who was paralyzed—'I say to you, rise, pick up your bed and go home.' And immediately he rose up before them and picked up what he had been lying on and went home, glorifying God" (Luke 5:24-25).

I'm grateful for the doctor who diagnosed and treated my pneumonia years ago. I'm thankful that Daddy saw my need and carried me to the hospital for help. And just like I needed my father to get me to the ones who could help me, sometimes we need the strength and faith of others to carry us to the healing arms of Jesus.

The good news is that, even though every ailment our bodies experience may not be healed on this side of heaven, our souls will always find healing in the presence of Jesus. And if we don't feel like we can get there on our own, we can ask God for friends who will help us come close to Him, trusting Him to bring wholeness to our hearts when we reach out in faith and enter His presence.

Pause:
Read Luke 5:17-26; Matthew 15:30; Psalm 33:9.

Ponder:
In what areas of your heart do you need healing? Then, think of a friend who may need healing and ask Jesus to provide healing for them, too.

Pray:
Dear Father, help me to be honest with friends in my life about where I need help coming to You. I also ask You to provide healing for my friends and family members who have hurting hearts today. May the lost be found in Your presence.
In Jesus' name, Amen.

DAY 34
Grace to Make It

And he said to her, "Daughter, your faith has made you well; go in peace."
(Luke 8:48)

When I was twenty-six years old, my body stopped functioning properly. I had to hug the wall for support when I walked, and I wore a towel wrapped around my neck to hold my head in an upright position. My muscles were too weak to perform daily tasks. After too many doctor visits to recall, I received a diagnosis of Fibromyalgia, Chronic Fatigue Syndrome, depression, and anxiety disorder.

For fifteen long years, my life was filled with a cycle of suffering and begging God for healing. But as nothing changed, my only hope was in knowing that I was a child of God and that He was with me in the pain.

When I think about the bleeding woman found in the gospel of Luke, I have to stop and wonder if she felt some of the same feelings of isolation, pain, and loss that I experienced. For twelve years, she also suffered from a seemingly incurable disease, until one day, she gathered the courage to step out in faith and reach for the robe of Jesus.

When her hand made contact with Jesus' garment, she was rewarded with immediate healing. Our sweet Jesus met her gaze and tenderly referred to her as His daughter: "Daughter, your faith has made you well; go in peace." Because of Christ's healing, this woman—now His daughter—was acceptable to God the Father.

In the original Greek, the word "daughter" in Luke 8:48 is *thygatēr.* As this woman became a "daughter of God," a term of endearment, it suggests that she is "acceptable to God" and can rejoice in God's particular care and protection.

Our acceptance by our Heavenly Father is based on Christ healing us, too. Although we may not be physically healed by Him here on earth, He has spiritually healed us by making the way to the Father possible (Isa. 53:4-5). And because of the ultimate, eternal healing, we can rejoice in knowing that no matter what we suffer—or for how long we suffer—He will provide the protection and grace that we need.

By God's grace, those torturous days of my chronic illness are now only a memory. Still, sometimes I can feel the weight of depression and anxiety resting heavily on me in difficult seasons. It is then that I recall Jesus' compassionate words to the bleeding woman and hear Him tenderly refer to me as His daughter. I can trust that His grace is always extended to me. Sweet sister, you can do the same.

PAUSE:

Read Luke 8:43-48; Isaiah 53:3-6; 2 Corinthians 6:18.

PONDER:

How can the truth of being God's daughter give you hope today in your current situation? List areas in your life where you need healing today and ask Him to help you trust Him for that healing.

PRAYER:

Dear Father, sometimes I struggle with believing I am Your daughter. Would You help me to hear Your tender voice speaking into my pain? Help me trust You for my care and protection. Please provide the healing I need. In Jesus' name, Amen.

DAY 35
Surrendering Healing to His Will

"For I am the LORD who heals you."
(Exodus 15:26c NKJV)

I sat with the mesh skin-toned braces secured tightly around each wrist. The metal pieces tucked down in each one relieved the pain and discomfort from carpal tunnel syndrome. But the relief was minimal: the braces hindered the ability to hold my Bible, turn its pages, and record Scriptures in my journal.

Carpal tunnel syndrome was an unwanted gift that came along with the other diagnoses that looted my life of independence and fullness during that season. And it frustrated me to no end. *Lord, I can't endure this, too. If You've brought me to sickness, I need to be able to spend time in Your Word and journal my thoughts. Please save me from this pain.*

Within a few days I needed the wrist braces less and less. Then, one day, I realized weeks had passed since I'd used them. I never needed them again.

I pleaded for Him to answer—and He did! And I'm still in awe of the Lord healing me.

But He hasn't always answered my prayers in such a miraculous manner. Even though I packed the wrist braces away quickly—and forever—my more debilitating ailments lingered for years. I don't understand why sometimes God chooses to heal immediately while tarrying other times. But it doesn't make Him less of a healer.

God promised healing to the Israelites if they would seek His face and obey His commandments: "If you diligently heed the voice of the LORD your God and do what is right in His sight, give ear to His commandments and keep all His statutes, I will put none of the diseases on you which I have brought on the Egyptians. For I am the LORD who heals you" (Exod. 15:26).

But this promise does not extend to the New Testament. The Church today cannot claim the full promise of "if they did this then that would happen" found in this verse. Yet, the good news we can hold to is that our Mighty God who was—and forever will be—our Father, holds the power to heal. And still does!

We witness this power in the healings performed by Jesus in the New Testament. He healed diseases (Matt. 4:23-24). He gave sight to the blind, made the lame walk, and the mute were able to speak (Matt. 15:30; Mark 7:31-37). And He even raised the dead (Luke 7:11-16; John 11:1-54).

The same God who revealed Himself as the healer of the Israelites—and by the powerful New Testament healings of Jesus—declares that He is a healer today. Healing may not come in the form we expect (or want).

It may not arrive in the timeframe we desire, but it will come.

Sweet soul, our Father will not withhold any good thing from us—even if we must wait until we step foot on the streets of gold. In the presence of the Lord, our healing is complete. Hallelujah!

Pause:
Read Genesis 15:22-27; Psalm 103:2-3; Romans 5:3-4.

Ponder:
In what situation are you asking the Lord for healing? How does knowing healing rests in the hand of your Father provide peace to your heart no matter the outcome this side of heaven?

Pray:
Dear Father, thank You for holding healing in Your hands. I trust Your timing for the healing I want—and I accept Your way is best. In Jesus' name, Amen.

DAY 36
Enduring to the End

He said to me, "My grace is sufficient for you,
for my power is made perfect in weakness."
therefore I will boast all the more gladly of my weaknesses,
so that the power of Christ may rest upon me.
(2 Corinthians 12:9)

God never audibly said no to me. But on the day I turned forty years old, the hope that swelled in my heart to have children one day wouldn't rise above the floor. Before that moment, I'd gripped expectation and pled with my whole heart for God to give me babies. As far back as I could remember I wanted five, but I resolved to settle for just one—it never happened.

Chronic illness stole my child-bearing years, and although forty is not too old to conceive, I knew my window of opportunity had slammed shut. This realization shook me with grief. Throughout that day, even during a surprise birthday party orchestrated by my husband, one question burned in my mind: *Why, God?*

Looking back on my fortieth birthday (over a decade ago)—the day I knew the Lord's answer to my prayer for children was no—I latched onto God's words to the Apostle Paul: "My grace is sufficient for you, for my power is made perfect in weakness" (2 Cor. 12:9a). And I've clung to them ever since.

Just like me, Paul received a no from God. Scripture describes Paul's asking the Father three times for healing from a thorn in the flesh (vv. 7-8). Yet after pleading with God, the answer was no to his request. And the Lord didn't say no because He was a mean ogre like the enemy might try to convince us.

God said no because He wanted to give Paul something greater than physical healing. He desired to bestow humility upon the apostle and to give *Himself*—His grace, power, strength, and sufficiency. The Father wants (and promises) to give us the same gifts.

Paul's prayer for healing didn't look like what he expected—and neither did mine. Paul's thorn remained and my womb stayed empty. Yet just as the Father extended grace to overcome the pain Paul endured, He offered the same grace to me as I buried a dream laying on an ash pile of culminated losses from years of sickness.

Perhaps you're seeking healing in your life. Can I gently suggest that you let go of expectations on how healing should look—or feel? Yes, our Father is able, capable, and sometimes He will heal us by removing the pain. Yet, He may choose to heal by giving us Himself. Ultimately, the Lord is the greatest healing we can ever receive—and His grace is sufficient to see us through until He calls us home to glory.

PAUSE:
Read 2 Corinthians 12:7-10;
2 Corinthians 13:4; Ephesians 3:16.

PONDER:
How does knowing that God's gift of His presence, power, and strength is the ultimate answer to healing bring comfort to your heart? Write down your requests for healing and ask the Father to give you grace to accept His answer, however He chooses to respond.

PRAY:
Dear Father, when the answers to my prayers for healing don't look like what I expect, my heart grieves. Help me trust that Your grace is sufficient for whatever weakness, pain, or heartache I experience. Fill my heart with the comfort of Your presence, power, and strength to overcome my struggles. In Jesus' name, Amen.

SECTION 10

A MERCIFUL FATHER

DAY 37
What I Don't Deserve

The LORD is compassionate and gracious,
slow to anger, abounding in love.
(Psalm 103:8)

"Do you know what Grandma did to me? She disciplined me!" I was four years old and had mistakenly expected my father to take my side. When I saw his brows lift in a questioning gaze, I immediately regretted opening my mouth.

"What did you do today that would make Grandma have to discipline you?" The question hung in the air, and although I tried back-pedaling, I couldn't avoid my daddy's gaze. The four walls of our tiny kitchen felt like they were closing in on me while Daddy grabbed the phone from the wall and dialed Grandma.

As I listened to the one-sided conversation, tears spilled over as I heard Daddy's tone grow in disappointment and frustration. That's where I became undone.

"I'm sorry, Daddy. I'll never do it again." It was all I could choke out.

Perhaps that day I wanted to turn the TV to my favorite show while she wanted to watch the news, or maybe I wanted to eat a treat that she said no to. Whatever it was, my grandmother had told me no, and I didn't want to hear it. I told her that if she didn't let me do what I wanted, I would get a stick and hit her. She still said no. Running out her front door and down the steps, I grabbed the first stick I found, and proceeded to smack Grandma's calves until she took the stick from me and popped my bottom in return.

It was no more than I deserved.

When I naively shared this account with Daddy, he rightfully decided to dole out his own correction. But something happened between Daddy's conversation with Grandma and my pleas for mercy. Shaking with tears, I felt Daddy's arms surround me. Gently, he pulled me into his arms and soothed my tears with a promise to withhold further punishment. And I can still hear him whisper, "I love you" in my ear.

In Psalm 103, King David points to the character of God. He describes Him as "compassionate and gracious, slow to anger, abounding in love" (v. 8). The truth is that we are clothed in flesh and constantly battle our sinful nature—even after salvation. Just like the four-year-old me, we want our own way and mess up trying to get it. For this, there is no defense.

Yet the good news is that our Heavenly Father opens wide His arms of love, welcomes us with compassion, and is quick to forgive. Because Christ has already paid the price for our sin, we no longer have to endure separation from God or eternal punishment. Instead, the Holy Spirit cleanses us and gives us the power to walk in freedom. Hallelujah, what a good and merciful Father He is to us!

PAUSE:

Read Psalm 103; Psalm 86:15;
Romans 5:20-21.

PONDER:

How does knowing that God is merciful comfort your heart? What does it look like to walk out this truth?

PRAY:

Father, thank you for Your compassion, mercy, and love. Help me see how You've administered grace to me when I didn't deserve it. Show me areas where I need to ask for Your forgiveness and renew my relationship with You.
In Jesus' name, Amen.

DAY 38

Because of Mercy, I Live

When the goodness and loving kindness
of God our Savior appeared, he saved us,
not because of works done by us in righteousness,
but according to his own mercy.
(Titus 3:4-5a)

Thump thump ... thump thump. I listened to my steady heartbeat through the stethoscope attached to the blood pressure cup pinching my arm. Per my doctor's instructions, I kept a daily log of my blood pressure in hopes that it would shed light on when—and why—it was running low.

As the sound echoed in my ears, I was awestruck by God's mercy and kindness. In all the years I've lived—half a century now—I've never once commanded my heart to beat or questioned whether it was beating. Each day of my life, I take for granted the fact that blood flows through my heart vessels and veins. Yet, there's nothing I could ever do to make my heart function. It's a gift of God's mercy and grace.

God's gift of salvation is the same.

In the Apostle Paul's letter to Titus, he states: "When the goodness and loving kindness of God our

Savior appeared, he saved us, not because of works done by us in righteousness, but according to his own mercy" (vv. 4-5a). Through the lovingkindness of our Father—and His great mercy—Jesus came to earth, suffered, died, and rose again to give us salvation.

And this is the way it had to be. The prophet Isaiah explained that human righteousness is "like a polluted garment" (Isa. 64:6). Any good you or I ever do can never be good enough. Any work we perform will never be sufficient to close the gap separating us from a Holy Father.

The good news is that it's not up to us. The mercy of God provided a way for us to live as one with the Father—to be cleansed from all unrighteousness and live a victorious life free from guilt and shame. Being justified by His grace, we are made heirs to the hope of eternal life (Titus 3:7).

We only have to accept it.

Sweet friend, may gratefulness for the lovingkindness of the Lord who created our hearts and commands them to function overflow from our lips. By God's grace, He gives us strength to behold the sun's rising and its setting.

May we be overwhelmed by the Lord's mercy that saves us and gives us the right to be heirs to His kingdom. What glorious joy, hope, and peace exist in knowing that one day—when our hearts beat for the last time on this side of heaven—we will be graciously welcomed into the presence of the Holy God, our Father. Hallelujah!

PAUSE:

Read Titus 3:3-7; Romans 3:24-31; Ephesians 2:4-9.

PONDER:

Looking back over the span of your life, how has God given you mercy physically, emotionally, and spiritually? Give the Lord thanks for all He's done, especially the gift of salvation.

PRAY:

Dear Father, thank You for Your grace and mercy that I could never earn, but You lovingly extend to me. I praise You for the gift of salvation. I'm grateful for every beat of my heart. And with joy, I look forward to the day I will join You in glory. In Jesus' name, Amen.

DAY 39

Finding Mercy in His Presence

Let us then with confidence draw near to the throne of grace, that we may receive mercy and find grace to help in time of need.
(Hebrews 4:16)

Tentatively, I stepped inside the metal-reinforced doors of the Pentagon. The grand entryway, canopied by high ceilings, seemed to swallow me as I walked beside my husband and our friends who prearranged the visit. We were met by security officers who required us to produce photo ID and confirmation of our tour's approval. Our small group was led by Pete, who worked at the Pentagon. Clad in his military uniform, he confirmed to the officer that he was sponsoring our tour.

Pete had the right to enter the Pentagon and—by his invitation—we were allowed past the gates. As our group proceeded down the vast corridors flanked by military regalia, photos of high-ranking government officials, and national memorials, I thought of all the VIP's sitting at their desks behind the closed doors we were passing. Not one of these people was available for me to walk into their presence and hold a conversation.

But there is One—the Lord Jesus—who is greater than any other, who gives us the right to enter His presence with boldness.

In Hebrews 4:16, the Apostle Paul declares: "Let us then with confidence draw near to the throne of grace, that we may receive mercy and find grace to help in time of need." It is the mercy (not getting what we deserve) of God and the grace (getting what we don't deserve) of our Lord that gives us an open invitation to run into the Father's presence.

May our hearts be in awe that the King of Heaven invites us to run to Him with our needs, thoughts, and desires. Our Father is not closed off from us and we never have to schedule an appointment to meet with Him.

Instead, we can enter into the presence of the Lord without hesitation or fear of rejection because He is always accessible and approachable. And in His presence we find mercy and grace sufficient for our needs.

I don't expect to visit the Pentagon again. And I'm sure many places in this world exist where I would never receive an invitation to visit. But that's okay, because you and I have access to the God of the Universe—our Father—who welcomes us to run into His presence any time, in any circumstance, and with any need. We have the assurance that He will meet us with both mercy and grace.

PAUSE:

Read Hebrews 4:14-16; Ephesians 2:18; 1 Peter 2:10.

PONDER:

What situation calls for your Father's grace and mercy today? Run into His presence with the assurance that He will welcome—and hear—you. Don't hesitate to ask Him for what you need.

PRAY:

Dear Father, thank You for inviting me into Your presence. Help me to enter in with boldness as I share my requests for help—and grace. Wholeheartedly, I praise You for Your never-ending mercy. In Jesus' name, Amen.

➳ DAY 40 ➳
Remember God's Goodness

"Thus far the LORD has helped us."
(1 Samuel 7:12 NKJV)

I have boxes filled with journals holding details about my life since my tween years. Most of the parchment-colored papers hold sincere prayers, hard questions, and struggles I felt I couldn't discuss with anyone except the Lord.

Recently, I pulled out a few of these journals and was dropped back into those valleys where I wondered if and how God would ever bring me through. One such place was the desert of isolation produced by years of chronic illness. I could feel the tears that stained the pages. My heart's desperate pleas for the Lord to bring change resounded across the entries. And I beheld, once again, those battles with disappointment, despair, and disillusionment.

But these aren't the only stories being written. I gaze back and see the Author penning a masterful narrative of my life—His presence walking beside me all along. I'm certain we all can look back over our lives and recognize this same pattern. How in God's mercy He held us, stayed with us, and carried us during the hardest times.

Perhaps we've come from paths of illness, fear, regret, and loneliness. Maybe we've lived through dysfunctional relationships, unfulfilled dreams, financial upheaval, and loss. Yet through it all, God's mercy sustains us—and it's by His goodness alone our lives are richer. It's important for us to pause and remember how the hand of our Father has led us in the valleys.

In the Old Testament, an Ebenezer stone was a rock of remembrance. God's people set an Ebenezer before them and declared: "Thus far the LORD has helped us" (1 Sam. 7:12). When they walked by the stone, it reminded them of God's victory—and His goodness in their lives. And the stone also pointed the Israelites to how the Mighty God of the past is the same God of the future. What the Lord has done before, He will do again.

Friend, whether in sickness or health, poverty or wealth, at home or abroad, through arduous times or ease, we've been helped by the gracious lovingkindness of our Father. Let's erect a monument in our hearts—and homes—to represent how the Lord has shown His merciful kindness to us.

As we remember our Father's faithfulness in every battle we face, it stirs our hearts to keep trusting Him now and evermore. Assuredly, thus far He has led us, and He will sustain us until the day He welcomes us home.

PAUSE:

Read 1 Samuel 7:9-14; Psalm 136;
Luke 1:50.

PONDER:

Make a list of the difficult places God has brought you from and praise Him for His unfailing mercy through it all. Revisit this list when your heart needs encouragement—and keep adding to it.

PRAY:

Dear Father, thank You for Your unending goodness. It's by Your mercy alone that I've made it through the trials in this life. Your lovingkindness overwhelms me. Wholeheartedly, I will praise You now and forevermore. In Jesus' name, Amen.

EPILOGUE
Holding Tightly to My Father's Hand

Rain splashed against my bedroom window and shook me from my slumber. Trembling from the night's lack of sleep, I untangled myself from the covers, swung my legs over the side of the bed and paused on its edge. Reality sank like a boulder in my heart, and I struggled to push air through my lungs. This was the day I would gather with my family to bury my daddy.

Through gushing tears, I managed to stumble into the bathroom, shut the door, and collapse on my knees. *I can't do it, Lord. Not this. I can't do this.* Curling myself into a ball, I wanted to stay there forever, even as hot tears glued my face to the cool tile floor. Any place was better than where I knew the day would take me.

Deep within the wells of my soul, I recognized that my capability for the task ahead was nonexistent. "I won't do it, Lord. I won't go." I croaked out my declaration. Then the Spirit whispered Philippians 4:8 to my spirit: "Finally, brothers, whatever is true, whatever is honorable, whatever is just, whatever is pure, whatever is lovely, whatever is commendable, if there is any excellence, if there is anything worthy of praise, think about these things."

I was swaddled in a warm blanket of comfort as the Lord prompted my soul to recall, rely on, and hold to the truth: the good and holy truth that God, in His sovereignty, could be trusted in every circumstance of my life. It's the same truth that He had continued to reveal to me since that day, almost three years before, when I sat in my counselor's office and admitted my struggle to trust the Lord. That had been the day the Spirit invited me to join Him on a journey to discover Him as my True Father—loving, good, kind, present, and able to provide for my every need.

It was the same comfort He had whispered to me just six days before: the night I received the call that Daddy had unexpectedly slipped into heaven. On December 17, 2020, after suffering with COVID in the hospital for eight days, suddenly Daddy stood in the Presence of his Maker. He bid this world goodbye, leaving a gaping hole in my heart—one that only Jesus could fill.

With my face still plastered to the floor, I began meditating on Philippians 4:8, and memories from the past few months rushed through my mind like scenes from a movie: the memory of visiting my father at his apartment and looking at sepia-colored photos with him while we recalled the good times our family had together throughout the years. The memory of witnessing my parents working out their marriage and making plans to reunite. And the memory of Daddy asking me for forgiveness, even as I admitted my own shortcomings to him—and both of us granting each other grace to move forward in our relationship with a newfound appreciation for one another.

All of these instances were true, yet there was an even greater truth threading through each memory: the truth of my Heavenly Father's presence and sanctification in situations I never would have chosen to walk through.

I realized that the only way my earthly father and I had been able to stitch back together what his substance abuse had shredded apart was by recognizing, relying on, and trusting in the goodness of my One True Father. In this, I was able to release my daddy from the expectations I had wrongly placed on him—including the expectation for him to be a *perfect* man without faults.

And now, by power from above, I would rejoice in the fact that Daddy was walking wholly alive—free from the suffering and pain of this world—in the Presence of his Heavenly Father. And although my heart grieved him, I would choose to continue placing my hand into the hand of this same Father who was reaching out to me.

Then I heard the Spirit whisper again. "Behold, I am with you always, to the end of the age" (Matt. 28:20b). There on the bathroom floor, knowing that I was not alone infused my body with the strength I needed to rise and face the heartbreaking reality of that day. The day that would lead me to the end of the earthly road I had traveled with Daddy.

* * *

Hours later, my husband parked the car outside my mother's family home place—the place I would stand with my family to say a final goodbye to the father who introduced me to Jesus. That morning's rain had dissipated but the sky continued to swell with gray clouds. It was a perfect reflection of my heart.

I began the trek down the muddy path that led to the family cemetery. And there, in the distance, I glanced at the sturdy mahogany casket that held the shell that was once Herculean to me—the body of my daddy. I pulled my woolen coat tighter and retied the belt to ward off the cold wind that whipped through the air, all while whispering a prayer. "Meet me there, Lord. Meet me there." With each step that my boots slogged through the mud, an other-worldly peace, comfort, and calm filled my soul as I heard the Spirit whisper His response: "*I am here*." And He certainly was with me.

My memories of my dad's memorial service are choppy. I don't recall the exact words that were spoken nor many details of who was in attendance. Shock does that to a person navigating loss and grief. But there's something that I have no doubt about: I was held and carried through the day by the mighty hand of my Heavenly Father—and He has continued to carry me ever since that day.

* * *

It has been four years since my daddy was ushered into his heavenly home, and six years since I sat in the counselor's office struggling to process the pain that set me on the path to knowing God as my True Father. I wish I could say that I've never had to battle doubt, fear, or mistrust in my faith since then. But that wouldn't be true. Yet when those internal wars have raged, I've been able to go to the Word and read the stories of David, Sarah, Moses, Paul, the bleeding woman, Jeremiah, and other saints of old—along with the words of Jesus Himself. I've witnessed how God revealed Himself as a loving, guiding, faithful, protecting, and trustworthy Father.

I've beheld the Father offering encouragement, comfort, healing, and mercy to His children in biblical times. And I've been able to trace His hand throughout my own life and witness my Heavenly Father show up in each of the same ways for me, over and over again. This is where I find assurance that what the Lord has done before, He will do again (Heb. 13:8). He is the same Father today as He was in days of old.

On this side of heaven, each of us will experience despair, doubt, and fear—particularly when those who should be the most trustworthy in our lives, fail us instead. When those who should have the highest regard for our hearts make choices that hurt, betray, or disappoint us, we're often left feeling unloved, unknown, and unseen. And though there's no excuse for wrongdoing, those wounds left by others open a door of opportunity.

It's an opportunity to run into the arms of the One—and only One—who never disappoints, harms, or forsakes us. Our Heavenly Father opens wide His arms to welcome us into His presence. Friend, I pray you rush into His presence now and forevermore.

After all, He is a trustworthy Father who loves, protects, provides, comforts, guides, heals, and encourages us through each step we take in this life. Our Father, in His faithfulness, extends mercy to us and uses every situation—good or bad—to bring us closer to Him and reveal Himself more fully to us. You will find that He is a perfect Father, able to fill every longing of your heart.

A PERSONAL INVITATION TO HAVE A RELATIONSHIP WITH JESUS

Perhaps you've journeyed with me through the pages of this book and witnessed the hand of the Father work on behalf of His children, but you don't recall the time when you entered into a relationship with Him: you're unable to refer to God as your Father. Let me assure you: He wants to call you His daughter, too. I'd like to invite you to join God's family because the door is open to you.

The path to salvation is a simple one:

Sin separates humanity from God. When Adam and Eve partook of the forbidden fruit in the garden, sin entered the heart of man. Therefore, we are all born into this world with our hearts bent toward sin. Romans 3:23 declares: "For all have sinned and fall short of the glory of God."

In our sin, we cannot reach God's glory and holiness on our own. We cannot be good enough, perfect enough, or righteous enough to make our own way to heaven. There is separation between us and God, but we cannot bridge it on our own strength. The Holy God had to bridge the gap between the hearts of humans and His own. The bridge is Jesus Christ.

Jesus lived the perfect life we could not and died in our place, taking our sin upon Himself as a sacrifice to pay for our sin for all time (Col. 2:13-14). His resurrection then proved His power over hell and the grave, paving the way for us to experience eternal life with Him, forever.

God did this because He loved us. Perhaps the most familiar Bible verse of all time is John 3:16: “For God so loved the world, that he gave his only Son, that whoever believes in him should not perish but have eternal life.” The good news of this Scripture is that God did all that was necessary to secure eternal life for us.

Without Jesus’ coming to earth, His death on the cross, and His resurrection, humanity would be forever doomed to hell—and eternal separation from God. Romans 6:23 tells us: “For the wages of sin is death, but the free gift of God is eternal life in Christ Jesus our Lord.”

God gave His only Son, Jesus, as the one-time payment for sin. But because love is not love if it’s forced, God does not require anyone to enter a relationship with Him. We get to choose.

Yes, salvation—and God’s love—is a free gift. But it’s a gift that must be received: "Behold, I stand at the door and knock. If anyone hears My voice and opens the door, I will come in to him and eat with him, and he with Me" (Rev. 3:20). The Lord is knocking on the door of your heart. Will you let Him come in?

You can have this gift by opening your heart to Jesus and inviting Him to come in today.

So, what are the steps to salvation?

1. Admit your need for salvation (Rom. 3:23).
2. Turn from your sins (Rom. 5:8).
3. Believe through faith that Jesus is the Son of the living God who died and rose again. And surrender to Him (John 3:16).
4. Accept this free gift of salvation by asking Jesus Christ to come into your heart and begin a new life with Him (Rom. 10:9).

You can start by praying a simple prayer like this from your heart:

Dear God, I know that I am a sinner. I know You love me, and I believe that Jesus is the Son of God who died for my sins and raised from the dead in victory over death. I now turn away from my sin and I ask Your forgiveness. Jesus, by faith I receive You into my life as my personal Lord and Savior. Come into my heart and take control of my life. I will follow you for the rest of my days. Thank You for saving me. In Jesus' name, Amen.

If you've made a decision to follow Christ, desire prayer, or would like more information, and live in the US, feel free to contact the Billy Graham 24/7 Prayer Line. The number is 855-255-7729 (855-255-PRAY).

You can also contact a Christian friend, visit a local church, and reach out to a pastor to go further in your faith. My prayers are with you, dear friend.

ACKNOWLEDGMENTS

The writing of this book is a wonder in the grace, joy, and faithfulness of my Lord Jesus. I'm grateful, honored, and humbled by the ability to present this book as a testimony of God's goodness. But this gift would not have been possible without the support, encouragement, and prayers of many others. Though the number of those who inspired and helped me is countless, I will attempt to cover a few. If you are one of those I fail to mention, it is unintentional—and I extend my deepest gratitude to you as well.

To **Rolland**—you, my dear husband, have held me up when my strength was gone. Thank you for calling me a writer—and believing in me—before I ever considered this writing life was even possible. I'm grateful for your support and love on this journey of life. Love you, always and forever!

To **my parents**—thank you for loving me, providing a strong foundation in Christ, and teaching me to love and serve well. I love you, Mama! Lord, tell Daddy that I love him too!

To the **Clarks**—thank you for showing me that family can be counted on in the good and bad times. It's a joy to do life with you all!

To **Abby and Aaron**—thank you for allowing this aunt to feel like a mother. I love you both with all my heart!

To the **team at Christian Focus Publications**—you are a dream come true. Thank you for your belief in this project and in me. I'm grateful to partner with you in kingdom ministry!

To **Ann Swindell**, my agent—I don't have words to express my appreciation for you, dear friend. So, I'll just say that I thank God for you, always. You've been a patient and thoughtful teacher. You've been a cheerleader, mentor, and friend. And you've knocked on doors because you believed in me and this project. Thanks for your faithfulness. I'm eternally grateful for you. Love you.

To **Jenny**—thank you for your thoughtful suggestions and editorial feedback on my terrible first drafts. I'm so grateful to have you as a friend and companion on this writing journey. Love you, dear friend.

To my Writing with Grace Mastermind friends—**Jenny, Emily, Christina, and Jo Beth**, thank you for your friendship, critiques, and championship. I thank God for allowing me to walk this writing path with you!

To my BGARC ladies—**Abigail, Amber, Christina, Donna, Kerri, Lindsay, and Melissa**—thank you for making my Wednesdays and Thursdays full of joy and purpose. I'm still amazed that I get to work with you. You have become family to me. Your support, prayers, and insistence on celebrating the small things has awakened my soul to the joy of the Lord. I love you all!

To the **Billy Graham Evangelistic Archive and Research Center team**—thank you for graciously welcoming me to use the invaluable resources of the research room. I'm both honored and humbled that I was able to peruse Billy Graham's books, commentaries, and sermon notes to gather ideas and information for this book. May the Lord continue to bless the work and ministry of the BGEA.

To **Greg and Pauline**—thank you for opening your home to me and Rolland. Your hospitality while I spent time writing in the Library of Congress was a gift I will never forget. I'm grateful for our friendship and pray God's blessings upon you both.

To **Pete**—thank you for sponsoring our tour of the Pentagon. May the Lord bless you for your kindness.

To **Katina and Ursulla**—thank you for being friends, confidants, and prayer partners for life. Your support is invaluable. Love you, my friends.

To **Jody**—my friend, I'm still in awe of God's gift of our friendship. I look forward to a lifetime of supporting one another with prayers and encouragement. Love you.

To my aunt, **Rosie Mae**—thank you for your encouragement, prayers, and selflessness. You have shown me Christ at every turn, and I'm beyond blessed to have you in my life. Your heart is gold! I know a rich reward awaits you in glory. Love you.

To the **Triune God: Father, Son, and Holy Spirit**—thank you for saving, rescuing, and keeping me. It is by Your grace, strength, and faithfulness alone that I live to tell the story of Your goodness. I'm honored that You would invite me to know You as my Father—and that You call me Your daughter. May You be glorified in all that I say and do. My heart is forever Yours!

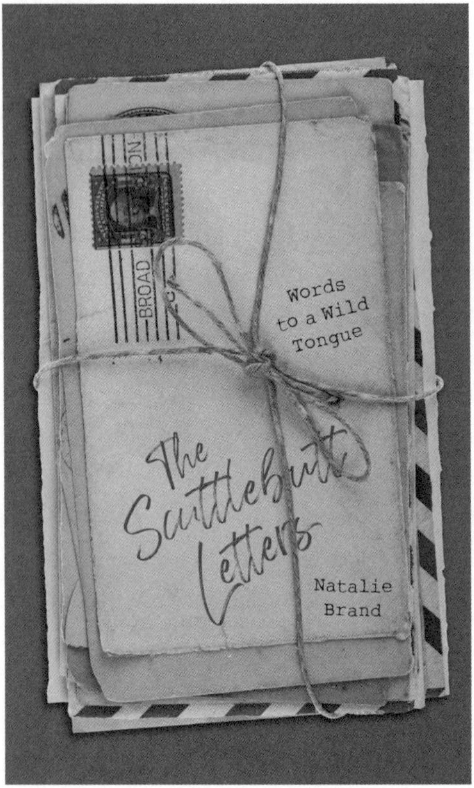

ISBN: 978-1-5271-1116-5

The Scuttlebutt Letters
Words to a Wild Tongue
Natalie Brand

- Follows format of *The Screwtape Letters*
- Letters from Heart to Tongue
- Hurt that can be caused by words

Scuttlebutt (naval slang for the ship's gossip) is the affectionate nickname given to the tongue by his correspondent in these letters. The letter–writer reprimands the tongue for steering the whole person into catastrophe, for enjoying little morsels of gossip, for creating smokescreens of lies. But it turns out that you can't change the tongue without changing the heart. And once the heart encounters the true Word, the tongue's words becomes even more important, as it becomes praisemaker, doxologist and theologian. An encouraging short book for anyone who struggles to keep their words under control.

Natalie Brand

Natalie Brand is a writer and Bible teacher. She has authored several books, including 'Priscilla, Where Are You? A Call to Joyful Theology' and 'The Good Portion: Salvation'. She has a Ph.D in systematic theology from the University of Wales and lectures in theology.

Christian Focus Publications

Our mission statement

Staying Faithful

In dependence upon God we seek to impact the world through literature faithful to His infallible Word, the Bible. Our aim is to ensure that the Lord Jesus Christ is presented as the only hope to obtain forgiveness of sin, live a useful life and look forward to heaven with Him.

Our Books are published in four imprints:

CHRISTIAN FOCUS

Popular works including biographies, commentaries, basic doctrine and Christian living.

MENTOR

Books written at a level suitable for Bible College and seminary students, pastors, and other serious readers. The imprint includes commentaries, doctrinal studies, examination of current issues and church history.

CHRISTIAN HERITAGE

Books representing some of the best material from the rich heritage of the church.

CF4KIDS

Children's books for quality Bible teaching and for all age groups: Sunday school curriculum, puzzle and activity books; personal and family devotional titles, biographies and inspirational stories – because you are never too young to know Jesus!

Christian Focus Publications Ltd,
Geanies House, Fearn, Ross-shire,
IV20 1TW, Scotland, United Kingdom.
www.christianfocus.com